TO:

_____

FROM:

_____

Give Yourself Some Grace

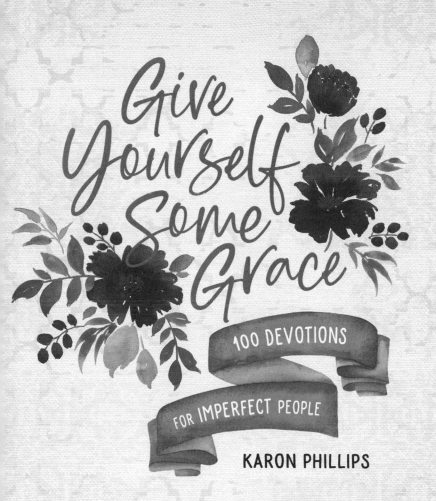

Give Yourself Some Grace

100 DEVOTIONS FOR IMPERFECT PEOPLE

KARON PHILLIPS

BARBOUR
PUBLISHING

ISBN 978-1-63609-254-6

Published by Barbour Publishing, Inc., 1810 Barbour Drive, Uhrichsville, Ohio 44683, www.barbourbooks.com

Our mission is to inspire the world with the life-changing message of the Bible.

Member of the
Evangelical Christian
Publishers Association

Printed China.

"CHRISTIANS AREN'T PERFECT, JUST FORGIVEN," THE SAYING GOES.

THAT'S TRUE, BUT MANY CHRISTIANS STRUGGLE TO ACCEPT BOTH THEIR OWN IMPERFECTIONS AND GOD'S FORGIVENESS.

This devotional will encourage imperfect Christians with the stories of imperfect people from the Bible. Learn from the accounts of men and women like:

- Sarah, who laughed at God's promise of a child
- John Mark, who deserted a missionary trip and caused a rift between Paul and Barnabas
- Peter, who failed and triumphed over and over.
- Martha, who was stressed out and irritable when Jesus was in her home
- two Pharisees, who followed Jesus secretly out of fear

The good news? Every one of them—and many like them—overcame their shortcomings to accomplish great things.

Give Yourself Some Grace shares two wonderful truths: you are not alone in your struggles, and God is always happy to forgive. Whatever your age or background, whatever challenges you're facing right now, you'll find encouragement in the pages ahead.

LET'S BEGIN WHERE WE ARE

"Christ Jesus came into the world to save sinners"—and I am the worst of them all. But God had mercy on me.

1 TIMOTHY 1:15–16 NLT

Paul should've been the last person on earth God used to reach anyone, let alone more than half the known world. He lived to kill those he chose because they chose Jesus. But that would end. On a dusty trade route on his way to more destruction, Paul was struck blind for three days and called to work against all he'd stood for. In immeasurable surprise his eyes were opened to the pure love of Jesus and "the incomparable riches of his grace" (Ephesians 2:7 NIV)—and he never looked back.

We see that in ourselves sometimes. We're quick to accept the blame of being what we feel is the "worst of all" that God has ever seen, then just as quickly freeze in unbounded surprise when He stops by with a job. But that's what the blinding light of Jesus' love does: opens our eyes to something else, a new life. He stops us so that we can begin.

The past remains while we go forward in undeserved

but never-ending grace, not perfect but perfected in His love to do the work that only a humble and redeemed believer can. Atop a history we can't erase, we build a future no one will forget. Because in the many people, places, and possibilities to come, we go as far as He says with powerful, traveling grace. And we're not alone.

Lord, thank You for taking my work-in-progress self and covering me in the shadow of Your love and grace. I accept the work You've planned for me. Let us begin.

COME ON IN—THE WATER'S FINE

"Yes, come," Jesus said. So Peter went over
the side of the boat and walked on the water
toward Jesus. But when he saw the strong wind
and the waves, he was terrified and began
to sink. "Save me, Lord!" he shouted.
MATTHEW 14:29–30 NLT

My heart just about explodes imagining the feeling Peter had walking on the water to meet Jesus, the bursting joy and overwhelming love in knowing that his Savior was calling to him and that His power would enable the impossible. So many amazing emotions must have surrounded Peter like a raft. . .but fear pulled him under.

Our own fear, doubt, and disbelief do terrible things to us all the time, paralyzing us and keeping us from trusting God. At that terrifying moment of reality, we feel our limitations too. I suspect Jesus wasn't surprised by Peter's stumble, and He's not surprised by ours. And just like Peter, we don't sink. Jesus' extended hand of grace snatches all unworthy but worthwhile souls, and we're safe to walk again.

Who knows what would've happened had Peter

kept walking on the water that night? It doesn't matter, because he *did* keep walking with Jesus and back to Jesus his whole life. Yes, he fell from time to time, but he learned to trust Jesus to catch him *every* time.

So can we. In that millionth of a second when the fear pushes out the faith just enough to make us weak, to trip us, to interrupt our walk, Jesus catches us and pulls us to Him, safe to step again.

Lord, Your grace overpowers
my fear and saves me
when I'm too afraid to move.
Help me always grab
hold of Your hand so we
walk wherever You say.

THE PRIVILEGE OF EXAMPLE

The king stood by the pillar and renewed the covenant in the presence of the LORD—to follow the LORD and keep his commands, statutes and decrees with all his heart and all his soul.
2 KINGS 23:3 NIV

Under the fifty-five-year influence of the evil king Manasseh, the people of Judah worshipped other gods, built idols, and completely forgot everything the Lord had told them. Then God found a faithful leader in young Josiah, who ordered that God's temple be repaired. Workers found the long-neglected "Book of the Lord," and Josiah began to both destroy and restore.

He removed and burned all the idols and leveled the shrines to the false gods. He smashed the altars and banished the fortune-tellers. He was no "do as I say, not as I do" kind of king. There would be no more pagan high places, and at the public reading and rededication of God's Word, "all the people pledged themselves to the covenant" (2 Kings 23:3 NIV). Then like a release after quarantine, the whole nation celebrated Passover in true and repentant reverence to God.

Because of Josiah's devotion, God spared the people during his reign. He lived his life in obedience and led by example. "Neither before nor after Josiah was there a king like him who turned to the Lord as he did—with all his heart and with all his soul and with all his strength" (verse 25 NIV).

Whether we lead a kingdom, a company, or a household, we set an example too. Repairing someone else's damage is hard, but with God's grace to fix what's wrong, we can turn a lot of hearts right.

Lord, make me a follower of You alone and a leader to everyone I know.

TROUBLED HEARTS, FULL HEARTS

"Don't let your hearts be troubled.
Trust in God, and trust also in me."
JOHN 14:1 NLT

Jesus' ministry and principles were sometimes hard for the young, headstrong disciples to fully understand. The Savior the world had waited for appeared without the expected military strength or traditional trappings of a king. Jesus was grace and love, asked for faith and following, and performed the signs the people wanted on His own timetable. As much as His disciples loved Him, they still got lost in their worry and doubt.

They saw the danger getting close; they feared for His life. . .and perhaps their own. Even with unlimited faith, they had limited understanding. But they taught us what to do with our questions—go to Jesus with them. What we don't understand is fully understood by Him, and His simple direction provides the confirmation, comfort, and peace we need.

We have full knowledge of the resurrection, but the disciples' troubled hearts needed assurance about the path they walked. As always, Jesus soothed them. "I am

the way, the truth, and the life. No one can come to the Father except through me" (John 14:6 NLT).

Jesus is the way to eternal life and earthly life better lived in His grace. Jesus is the truth of God and all He promised, forgiving us and loving us always because He said He would. Jesus is the living light of love, hope, compassion, and faith that forever fills the darkness. And when we fill our hearts with Him, they are troubled no more.

Lord, I will follow Your way and trust in Your truth so that Your light may shine through me and onto others.

THE FIGHT IN THE DOG

"The Lord doesn't see things the way you see them. People judge by outward appearance, but the Lord looks at the heart."

1 Samuel 16:7 NLT

The time had come to anoint a new king over Israel, and God sent His prophet Samuel to Jesse in Bethlehem. Jesse had eight sons, and when Samuel saw Eliab, the firstborn, he thought the young man was God's choice because of his impressive appearance. But God said no. When Samuel then asked to see all the sons, Jesse didn't include the youngest, who was busy tending the sheep. Jesse too was mistaken, but when he finally brought the little shepherd boy to Samuel, no one was mistaken anymore: "And the Spirit of the Lord came powerfully upon David from that day on" (1 Samuel 16:13 NLT).

As the old adage goes, it's not the size of the dog in the fight but the size of the fight in the dog that matters. God puts His spirit, His unbelievable and unexpected fight and power, grace and abilities—His *heart*—in us all. It's there to be discovered and never discounted. Every one of us has something to give back to God in

what we do with this life.

Samuel and Jesse were quick to see their errors and recognize God's will. May we be too. Because the Lord looks at the heart, let us examine our hearts and with every beat become more pure, more receptive, more full of the right kind of fight. And let us cheer each other on.

Lord, prevent me from discounting anyone or anything You've touched, including me. Help me be the believer You're searching for and see in others what You see in them.

THE ASTONISHING RANGE OF GRACE

The voice spoke to him a second time, "Do not call anything impure that God has made clean." . . . Then Peter began to speak: "I now realize how true it is that God does not show favoritism but accepts from every nation the one who fears him and does what is right." . . . The circumcised believers who had come with Peter were astonished that the gift of the Holy Spirit had been poured out even on Gentiles.

Acts 10:15, 34–35, 45 NIV

On a rooftop in the city of Joppa, God taught Peter a lifelong, universal lesson: Jesus is Jesus to everyone. Do we represent Him that way?

Peter was schooled in the law of dietary restrictions and cultural division, and while praying he saw a vision of all kinds of foods. He learned from this vision that if God made it, God loves it. Food was a metaphor. The keepers and teachers of the law resisted anyone different from them, including the uncircumcised Gentiles. But Jesus has no limits. He wants us free from limits too.

The new leaders of the faith had to break old habits

and learn the true inclusive love of Christ. If we've questioned someone's faith or resisted showing them ours because they come from somewhere else or don't think the way we do, then maybe we need a vision. Maybe we need to see more clearly like Peter did. Let us love and care with the reckless embrace of our Savior. His love that reaches rooftops, living rooms, and realms unknown is the love of a pure grace open to all.

Lord, help me see the way
Peter did with his eyes
closed and love the way You
do with my heart open.

PROMISE MADE, PROMISE FULFILLED

*"The least of you will become a thousand,
the smallest a mighty nation. I am the
Lord; in its time I will do this swiftly."*

ISAIAH 60:22 NIV

Despite coming defeat, captivity for seventy years, and episodes of disobedience and despair, the nation of Israel would rise again. What an encouragement to us when we give too much credence to our past and hurts!

Instead of looking forward and doing their best for God in everything to come, the Israelites were wallowing in what they couldn't change. But we don't have to relive our mistakes when God's grace releases us from them. Messy worlds call for mighty people, and that's us.

We're never too small or too late to become what God has designed. He claims us as the work of His hands and the shoots He's planted (Isaiah 60:21). We're right where we belong.

With this power of restarts and renewals, God says we'll "know that I, the LORD, am your Savior, your

Redeemer" (verse 16 NIV). That's grace to go and go again, to endure and elevate to something better.

Let us trust not only God's forgiveness but also His timing. And let's talk the way He often does—in past tense, as if something has already happened because He said it will. Every promise He's made is a promise manifested in the lives of those He loves. We *became* mighty, just the way God said.

So no matter how deep the hole of hopelessness we're in now, it became a hill of hallelujah we stood on and praised our Lord.

Lord, please help me trust
Your opinion of me and
Your timing to restore me,
mighty and redeemed.

GRACE BEARS INTEREST

"Or suppose a woman has ten silver coins and loses one. Won't she light a lamp and sweep the entire house and search carefully until she finds it? And when she finds it, she will call in her friends and neighbors and say, 'Rejoice with me because I have found my lost coin.' In the same way, there is joy in the presence of God's angels when even one sinner repents."

LUKE 15:8–10 NLT

As joyous as the woman in the story is, Jesus says to think bigger. That's God when He welcomes one of us to Himself with great joy. Like that lost coin, we're lost in fear, hopelessness, despair, disbelief, anger, waywardness, rebellion, and more. But He never gives up the search-and-rescue mission.

We wonder why the Pharisees Jesus was addressing wouldn't want that same love. Wouldn't they want to know that kind of value, the real worth that moves God in heaven to act? All they had to do was look at the "found coins" among them to see how it works and receive the grace for themselves. What's possible for one found soul is provided for us all.

While the Pharisees condemned Jesus for keeping company with the people they considered inferior, those very people found the God the Pharisees couldn't understand. His love for us, as imperfect and misplaced as we are, is only made better when others see and want it for themselves. Let us be found, hugged close, cherished, and celebrated while the world watches His grace come alive.

Lord, please come get me when I stray, and remind me of Your welcoming grace that covers me and spills onto others too.

ALWAYS LOOKING FORWARD

"Don't ask me to leave you and turn back.
Wherever you go, I will go; wherever you
live, I will live. Your people will be my
people, and your God will be my God."

RUTH 1:16 NLT

Naomi had lived east of Bethlehem, across the Jordan River in Moab, all her adult life, and there she buried her husband and two sons. Bitter and angry at God, she moved back home to Judah, but she didn't go alone. Despite the pain Naomi had endured, and even if she just wanted to go home to die in her hopelessness and anger, God had other plans.

When we're hurting, it's easy to blame God. But we're never done with our work until He says so, and the results are always beyond our expectations. Naomi's daughter-in-law Ruth went with her to Judah, and from there, Naomi guided Ruth to Boaz, helping grow the family tree of Jesus.

God's abundant grace shows throughout the story. It first led Ruth to trust her future to her faithful mother-in-law and accept the God she didn't know before. Then Ruth trusted Naomi even more and harnessed her own courage to approach the wealthy and powerful, generous and honorable Boaz. They married and became parents of Obed, grandparents of Jesse, great-grandparents of David.

Naomi's rekindled faith and obedient actions banished her bitterness and she "took the baby and cuddled him to her breast. And she cared for him as if he were her own" (Ruth 4:16 NLT). Naomi's pity of her past became part of Israel's force of the future.

Lord, please turn my self-pity into power fueled by Your grace and restore me to do my part in Your plan.

HE MEETS US AT OUR WELL

Then, leaving her water jar, the woman went
back to the town and said to the people, "Come,
see a man who told me everything I ever did.
Could this be the Messiah?" They came out of
the town and made their way toward him.

JOHN 4:28–30 NIV

Am I the woman at the well, so in need of grace but too
empty of hope to believe it exists for me? Or am I one
of the other "more righteous" women who judged the
outcast and saw no possibility of redemption for her?
Either way, the words about Jesus are for me. And you.

Hope is waiting in Him, to be poured out on our
hearts that are so dry and scorched from the absence
of His touch, hearts that are renewed and released
for so much more when His grace floods us like a
well overflowing.

The lone Samaritan woman went a long way to the
well, carrying a pail and her shame. There she met Jesus,
whose response isn't condemnation but construction,
not rejection but redemption, not forsaking but forward
moving. "Do something with what you now know and

others will make their way toward Me too," He says. The justification comes with a job.

The woman was a changed person, and those who shunned her before couldn't help but believe her raw, revealing testimony. Her shameful life now awash in unexpected blessing showed them that God's grace is not carved out only for those who aren't too far gone. It's the bottomless favor of His boundless love. Let's meet Jesus at our well. Let's bring others there too.

Lord, I run quickly to where You wait to meet me and make me whole with Your grace.

STAKE YOUR CLAIM, DO YOUR JOB

So Joshua said to the Israelites: "How long
will you wait before you begin to take
possession of the land that the LORD, *the*
God of your ancestors, has given you?"

JOSHUA 18:3 NIV

How long will we wait to get on with the life waiting for us? Sometimes we just want things to be easy because, let's face it, change is always hard. Life for the wandering Israelites wasn't without danger and chance after the move into the promised land.

Several of the tribes had stayed in more hospitable lands, and the house of Joseph—to Ephraim and Manasseh—still feared the Canaanites with their iron-plated chariots. But Joshua had led them there, and he knew that God had not brought along a single soul who didn't have a destiny in the new land.

So Joshua fired them up like a coach before homecoming, providing both encouragement and instruction, and they moved in God's grace. We can't be passive and wait for just the right time, because conditions are never perfect, but we are prepped by the God who directs all.

To the house of Joseph, Joshua said, "Remember who you are," and to the others, he said, "Remember what is yours."

To all of us who procrastinate today, who settle for less and fear the unknown, he says, "Get to work!" And God takes our wait and turns it into a stake to claim all that's ours.

Lord, please help me overcome my fear and hesitancy when we have work to do. Let's move when You say.

THE EARTHQUAKE'S FOR US

The jailer called for lights, rushed in and fell trembling before Paul and Silas. . . . "Sirs, what must I do to be saved?" They replied, "Believe in the Lord Jesus, and you will be saved—you and your household." Then they spoke the word of the Lord to him and to all the others in his house.

ACTS 16:29–32 NIV

Paul and Silas sat in jail in Philippi for preaching about Jesus. They were singing and praying when an earthquake shook open the doors and loosened the chains of all the prisoners. The jailer awakened to the fear that everyone had escaped, and he was about to kill himself because of it. Paul stopped him and saved him at the same time. In the wake of a miracle, he was face-to-face with an aching heart hungry for Jesus.

The jailer could've simply run away or put the prisoners back in the cells, but he saw the new beginning offered to him. And he took it. He brought Paul and Silas home with him and tended their wounds. He brought his new, unbound belief with him too. "He was filled with joy because he had come to believe in

God—he and his whole household" (Acts 16:34 NIV).

Formerly a part of the system to stop the news of Jesus, the jailer believed and became a part of the faithful to spread the news of his Savior. He started at home. When we see that kind of opportunity, let us not run away either. The world is still shaking with God's grace. Let's believe and be an example to others. Let's not miss the earthquake.

Lord, help me respond to any upheaval that makes me seek You. Then help me bring others along to see.

LOVE IN LISTENING, LOVE IN LABOR

Mary. . .sat at the Lord's feet listening to what he said. But Martha was distracted by all the preparations that had to be made. She came to him and asked, "Lord, don't you care that my sister has left me to do the work by myself? Tell her to help me!" "Martha, Martha," the Lord answered. . . . "Mary has chosen what is better, and it will not be taken away from her."
LUKE 10:39–42 NIV

We've all been Martha—the workaholic, employee of the year, and prize-winning volunteer, full of responsibility, efficiency, and fairness. Good qualities all, but second to first-place devotion to Jesus.

While Mary, Martha's sister, sat at Jesus' feet and ignored the work to prepare for guests, Martha kept working, maybe listening with one ear to Jesus' words but obsessing over Mary's choice, eventually asking Him to intervene. Her focus on the work was admirable, but her understanding of the moment was lost. We've been there.

Jesus gently corrected Martha, but only when she asked for help. Perhaps that's the lesson here. We should

check our focus with Jesus when we're busy so that we don't miss what Mary knew. What's the better use of our time and attention? Yes, our genuine hospitality and service is worship and a reflection of Jesus, and He loves us and others through that. Then sometimes He just wants us to sit with Him and listen to His words. We can do both. Martha did, serving a meal to Jesus as He prepared to enter Jerusalem on Palm Sunday (John 12:2), the devotion in her heart set before the dinner on her table.

Lord, I want to be Mary and Martha too—at the same time loving You with worship and work and showing that love to others.

TOO MUCH TO WIN

*When the angel of the L*ORD *appeared to Gideon,
he said, "The L*ORD *is with you, mighty warrior."*
JUDGES 6:12 NIV

God likes to do things His way. Gideon learned that.

Meeting an angel of God under an oak tree, Gideon complained about the conditions the Israelites were living in, overrun and pushed around by the Midianites. But the angel had a message for Gideon. In today's jargon, we could say the angel told him to "be the change you want to see." Except Gideon didn't feel anything like the "mighty warrior" God saw.

We've asked God our own "But how can I save Israel?" (Judges 6:15 NIV) question from time to time too. We've wondered if we have the strength, wisdom, and ability to do what He says to do, or if we heard the charge right in the first place. That's because we have to catch up to God's big plans sometimes, mixing belief into the grace He's supplied for the work.

To be sure about God's plan, Gideon asked for proof. Twice. And with the tolerant indulgences of a loving Father, God obliged. He then told Gideon his army

was too big, a seemingly good condition when going to meet your enemy. But fully believing now, Gideon followed God's orders and reduced his fighting force from 32,000 to 300 and won the battle because God said he would. God didn't need 32,000 soldiers to accomplish His goal. He needed one faithful follower.

It's hard sometimes to trust the quiet voice only we hear, but God's promises are lived out loud in our lives. Let us know Him so intimately that we can be nothing but absolutely sure of what we hear Him say.

Lord, please forgive my shaky faith when so much depends on me. Help me hear, trust, and obey.

STRENGTH FOR ALL THINGS

I know how to live on almost nothing or with everything. I have learned the secret of living in every situation, whether it is with a full stomach or empty, with plenty or little. For I can do everything through Christ, who gives me strength.

PHILIPPIANS 4:12–13 NLT

Discomfort is never welcomed. None of us want to be in want of anything, and in our download-it-now world, the idea of waiting through a difficult time is unbearable. In that frustration, we may make bad choices, ruled by the creature comforts we're missing and completely lost to walk through it all.

But Paul found favor in the walk.

How did he learn that? How long did it take him to focus on Christ as he taught and worked in difficult conditions? How often did he focus on what he lacked and struggle to represent Christ in dry seasons? And did he ever get too comfortable when "living in plenty" and forget that the company of Jesus is what truly matters?

Paul tells us he's walked through the same conditions

we're familiar with, and we can know he met Jesus on the way. For those in Philippi and for us, he points out the secret he's learned—Jesus the Source is always the same, providing strength and guiding our choices, regardless of what we have or don't have, because we walk with Him. The supply is never the question, and grace is always the answer.

Jesus will meet us on the way too. Let Paul's worst-kept secret be our best-loved guide.

Lord, please help me do all things without complaint and in the full strength of Your grace alone.

THE GRACIOUSNESS OF REST

*This is what the Sovereign LORD, the Holy
One of Israel, says: "Only in returning to
me and resting in me will you be saved. In
quietness and confidence is your strength."*
ISAIAH 30:15 NLT

Faster, harder, planning, scheming, go, go, go—"I have to!" No wonder we're tired. We fight first and listen later.

The Jewish leaders lost sight of who was in charge and replaced their faith with faulty plans. Facing a threat from Assyria, they made a treaty with Egypt for their protection. God wasn't pleased, because He wanted them to trust Him and Him alone to guide them through any danger. Bigger armaments, faster horses, and political maneuvers were not the answer. The harder the Israelites worked on their own, the more at risk they became.

It's the same with us. In trying relentlessly to find effective strategies for attacking our enemies, we expend all the power and strength we value so much. We're exhausted, empty, and lost. But God whispers, *"Let's start again. I'll take over now."*

God doesn't need our pointless activity—He wants

our perfect attention. And when we take a breath of Him, His graceful response is peaceful rest, one of His greatest gifts. In our rest we turn to Him.

Each night as I lay my head down, I say, "I rest and renew in love, trust, and expectation." It's my way of reminding myself of God's love that never ends, my trust in Him that keeps me going, and the wonderful expectation of all He's planning for us to do together. Quiet strength is found in Him when we renew in graceful rest.

Lord, please take away my rebellion and replace it with Your rest. I know we have much to do.

WEAK FLESH, STRONG SAVIOR

*Then he returned to his disciples and found them
sleeping. "Couldn't you men keep watch with
me for one hour?" he asked Peter. "Watch and
pray so that you will not fall into temptation.
The spirit is willing, but the flesh is weak."*

MATTHEW 26:40–41 NIV

The disciples who loved and followed Jesus to the end
fell asleep in an hour. They were tired, of course, and
needed rest as we all do, but this was not a story about an
ill-timed nap. Jesus woke and warned them about failing
to "keep watch" for the temptation they would face.

Following Jesus in this fallen and distracting world
requires vigilance and resistance. We've surely failed
plenty of times too because our flesh is weak. Jesus
knows that so many things—things like fear, fatigue,
and other people and their ideas—threaten to hurt us
and draw us away from Him. He says that being aware
is the first step. So let us know the enemy in whatever
form it appears and rely on His grace to overcome it.

Jesus knew that the plot to arrest and kill Him was
about to unfold, and He knew His disciples would

quickly feel the weight of the opposition that threatened to derail His church. He used their lapse as a lesson about all the bad in the world so they'd understand and "watch and pray," so they'd be alert to the evil and able to avoid it. Let us learn the lesson too.

My morning whisper of "I awake and arise in abundance, joy, and gratitude" now beckons me to be awake and aware, to fight and follow through every day.

Lord, please help me keep watch with You as Your grace gives me strength in my weakness.

TWO IS EVERYTHING, TWO THOUSAND NOTHING

A poor widow came by and dropped in two small coins. "I tell you the truth," Jesus said, "this poor widow has given more than all the rest of them. For they have given a tiny part of their surplus, but she, poor as she is, has given everything she has."

LUKE 21:2–4 NLT

Bowls for collections were in the front and the back of the temple, and the Pharisees enjoyed making a big show of their contributions, probably expecting Jesus to be impressed along with everyone else. Instead, He chose to focus on the smallest donation of the day—and the most valuable because it came from the pure heart of a true believer.

The Pharisees could give so much more than the widow, but the amount wasn't the point. Then and now what matters is the attitude of the giver. Have we ever lost sight of our giving of time, talent, or resources while growing accustomed to public praise?

Jesus says anything we do is a part of our relationship with Him, either for surrender or for show. All giving, growing, and work becomes worship when our motives are pure. Let us examine our hearts, seek God's direction, and give whatever we have for His use. His grace will bless that and provide more.

Maybe we're witnesses to this story of faith so that we have an example to emulate, not an act to embarrass us if we've not done the same. Maybe it's His way of helping us see that all giving starts in the heart and that where we've failed, He will guide.

Lord, help me remember that You want my whole heart, and whatever flows from it will be enough.

ALL THINGS NEW, ALL NEW THINGS

"Forget the former things; do not dwell on the past. See, I am doing a new thing! Now it springs up; do you not perceive it? I am making a way in the wilderness and streams in the wasteland."

ISAIAH 43:18–19 NIV

When the Israelites were trapped in Babylon, they grew weary and doubtful, feeling abandoned and heartbroken for all they had lost. Their homeland was a distant heartache, a seventy-year-old memory. They relived the assault of the Babylonians every time they gathered for worship in the pagan and hostile land. But God had not abandoned them. They were dwelling on the past, but He was already way ahead.

We can understand their despair. It's easy to get trapped in the past and see no hope for anything resembling a renewal, a revival, a reason to keep going. But when we're captive to whatever separates us from where we want to be, God sees far ahead to where *He* wants us to be.

Maybe a return is more of a restart, a chance to welcome Him anew into our hearts and create something

better than before. That's what He wanted with the Israelites. They had turned their hearts away from Him plenty of times before. Whether we admit it or not, so have we. But God's grace is abundant and His understanding of our flaws complete. He knows us well yet still believes there's more of His Spirit in us than our flesh. So we get another chance. Let's not waste it. New things await our return.

Lord, help me look ahead, trust Your preparation, and splash through the desert streams to new depths with You.

FIGHTING FOR THE WAY

"So my advice is, leave these men alone. Let them go.
If they are planning and doing these things merely
on their own, it will soon be overthrown. But if it is
from God, you will not be able to overthrow them.
You may even find yourselves fighting against God!"

ACTS 5:38–39 NLT

In Jerusalem, Peter and the other apostles were growing the church, and followers were spreading out everywhere. That kind of popularity and influence annoyed the Sadducees, so in their jealousy, they had them arrested. But when an "angel of the Lord" opened the cell doors, the apostles went straight to the temple to teach more about Jesus.

And then Gamaliel intervened. A teacher of the law and honored Pharisee who had taught Paul, he advised leaving the men alone. Perhaps his law-limited view was about to lead him and others to a new fulfilling faith. *Trust God*, he seems to say, *even when it's something new and unknown. Let's just watch how God could be working instead of clinging to our own reasons for opposing this new church of Jesus.*

It was a bold stand, and surely God's grace rested on Gamaliel the Pharisee to help him help Peter and the others continue their ministry.

Have we ever given in to the group around us, just to keep our place because we're comfortable or dependent on the inclusion? It's easier, but is it best? When God shows us the better way, let us have the courage of Gamaliel to stand up for His will triumphing over all. When the fight comes, let us choose the right side.

Lord, please make me bold and brave to go against the group when I need to and to trust Your control of the results.

NEW IN CHRIST

Imitate God, therefore, in everything you do,
because you are his dear children. Live a life
filled with love, following the example of Christ.
EPHESIANS 5:1–2 NLT

Do you know someone who struggles to get ahead of a bad past and live free in the grace of Jesus? Is it you? Are you your old lost self, living in shame or regret, or are you your new Jesus-found self, living free in reclamation and redemption?

The Christians in Ephesus (modern-day Turkey) had an ugly past of idol worship that led to bad behavior against each other and God. Then they turned to Jesus and had a whole new world opened up for them. But they were struggling to become the new while still ashamed of and participating in the old. "So stop," Paul told them. "Stop," he tells us. "Choose the new, choose Jesus—because it's your job to be just like Him."

The grace of God says to move on, leave the hurtful ways behind, and be an example instead. History is not disqualifying; it's just done. Like a broken stained-glass window, we let Jesus shine through the cracks so that all anyone sees in our lives is Him: "For you were once darkness, but now you are light in the Lord. Live as children of light" (Ephesians 5:8 NIV).

Paul wrote from prison to help the Ephesians see they had a second chance, a new life in Christ, a chance to build and reveal a bright future. God's grace makes it possible for all of us.

Lord, please help me be the light! Help me imitate You so that others want to shine as well.

GOD'S BLESSING IS BIGGER
THAN ALL THE REST

*"I am with you and will watch over you wherever you
go, and I will bring you back to this land. I will not
leave you until I have done what I have promised you."*
GENESIS 28:15 NIV

The story of twins Jacob and Esau is complicated, and
both failed in their own way. But God's plan didn't.

As a young man, Esau—the older brother by a heel—
traded his birthright as the firstborn for food Jacob
prepared. We'll never know if that contract would've
been enforced, because Jacob went a step further.

At his mother Rebekah's urging, he pretended to be
Esau and brought food to his father, Isaac, who was too
sick and blind to know the difference. Jacob lied when
Isaac asked if he was really Esau, and Isaac passed to
him the world-changing blessing of abundance, favor,
and power.

When we put our selfishness and ego above others
and what belongs to them, we too carry the burden Jacob
did. He was hated by his brother, who planned to kill
him, and lived with the knowledge that he had cheated

his father out of blessing his elder son. And because he knew he'd done wrong, Jacob spent the rest of his life trying to do right, fortified by a dream in which God promised the blessing of "all peoples on earth" through him (Genesis 28:14 NIV).

Jacob heard God, claimed that promise of companionship and help, and set about making it come true. The father of twelve tribes began with a grip on his brother and lived unashamed with God's grip on him.

Lord, please help me do things Your way and forgive me when I fail. Please watch over me and make me something good wherever I am.

CHOOSE WELL, MAKE THINGS BETTER

Esau ran to meet him and embraced him,
threw his arms around his neck, and
kissed him. And they both wept.
GENESIS 33:4 NLT

In Esau's earlier story, we see a reckless, impulsive, vindictive brother of Jacob running off to marry a Canaanite woman to spite his mother and father. We find someone quite different years later when Jacob decides to return home.

Esau had vowed to kill Jacob for stealing their father's blessing, and they hadn't seen each other since. In full remembrance and shame and facing retribution, Jacob brought gifts and bowed down to Esau, but the brother he met was a new man too.

Forgiveness, acceptance, redemption. Esau had repented and atoned for his mistakes. Then when he had the opportunity to respond to his brother, he passed on what he had received. In the valley there was healing in their tears.

That's the takeaway for us. Sure, we're often tempted, and we may even have the high ground and the advantage to carry out the retribution we feel we're entitled to. But that kind of revenge helps nothing. Searching for something that does help is the better choice. Then God graces us with the ability and inclination to do better, and we can reflect that grace onto others.

No matter how many years pass, and no matter the condition of the heart of the person who's wronged us, it's our call when we meet in the valley of Seir. Let us choose well.

Lord, I know that forgiveness comes from Your generous heart. Please help me pass it on and be a surprise blessing to others.

HE STILL FINDS US

"Nazareth!" exclaimed Nathanael. "Can anything good come from Nazareth?"
"Come and see for yourself," Philip replied.
JOHN 1:46 NLT

Nathanael's scoff—that nothing good could come from Jesus' hometown, including the Messiah Himself—has become catchall jargon for anything we easily discount. It's a judgmental retort made out of our prejudice, and it can be especially damaging when we turn it inward. Sometimes we ask the same question about ourselves because of where we've been or what we've done. "Can anything good come from *me*?"

It's hard going out into the world carrying our unbecoming baggage, knowing we will be judged by a past we can't change and won't be trusted to live a future we can't prove. We fear that we'll never overcome the life we've lived even if we feel far removed from it in our hearts.

But Jesus makes overcoming possible. He told Nathanael, "I could see you under the fig tree before Philip found you" (John 1:48 NLT), and He sees us too.

With full knowledge of everything we are and from the abundance of His grace, He sends someone to tell us who He really is. New life in Him is waiting for us because indeed something good has come.

Trusting his friend Philip, Nathanael went to see Jesus—and then dropped to his knees in the presence of his Savior. That's the faith and belief Jesus knows we're made of, and anything before is just gravel we trample over to get to Him.

Let us be the example of a restored life so that the Philips of today call their friends and say, "Come and see. Come and see the grace of God for yourself."

Lord, see me and walk with me—to overcome the past and celebrate the future.

CHANNELING COMMITMENT, FOLLOWING IN FAITH

*Then Simon Peter drew a sword and slashed
off the right ear of Malchus, the high priest's
slave. But Jesus said to Peter, "Put your sword
back into its sheath. Shall I not drink from the
cup of suffering the Father has given me?"*

JOHN 18:10–11 NLT

It's easy to label Peter impulsive and reactive, but we
can be the same way. And how many of us would've
wanted to do the same thing Peter did in the garden
of Gethsemane, to protect our Teacher out of love
and instinct?

But it's Jesus who protects us, and He wouldn't let
anything interfere with what He knew would happen
next. He had avoided capture up to that point and
could've avoided it then too, but instead He allowed it.
Peter, so passionate yet still struggling to understand
the long-range plan, could only see the immediate act,
which sprang loose the protector in him. Jesus had to
reprimand him, but He also recognized a raw response
prompted by deep devotion when He saw one.

Out of unbiased grace, Jesus healed Malchus's ear. And with Peter in check, He went back to His work and Peter went on to learn and grow stronger. Let us harness our temper and give great thought to our actions so that we help instead of hinder Jesus' work. (He may not always repair the ear we sever.) Let us learn to trust the plan we can't see or understand and allow God's grace to guide our reckless thoughts toward thought-out responses.

Lord, may my impulse always be to defend You, even though You don't need it. But please direct my sword where You choose.

GO BACK, GO FORWARD, KEEP GOING

When the LORD saw that he had gone over to look, God called to him from within the bush, "Moses! Moses!" And Moses said, "Here I am."

EXODUS 3:4 NIV

We're all capable of getting angry about injustice, feeling inadequate for big jobs, and running away from confrontation. But if God has a plan, our best response is to say, "Here I am," and to let Him sort out the details.

A Jew raised in Egypt, Moses killed an Egyptian foreman for beating a Hebrew slave. Pharaoh wanted Moses captured, so Moses ran east to Midian, became a shepherd, married, and lived forty years in exile. Then from flames in a bush on holy ground, God ordered him to return to Egypt and lead His people to a new land and a new life.

What was Moses' response? "Who am I that I should go to Pharaoh and bring the Israelites out of Egypt?" (Exodus 3:11 NIV). *I'm an old, stuttering fugitive,* he thought. *Surely God can find someone better.*

But no. . .God just provides the grace to get us through. How many times have we forgotten the power of that grace and struggled with tasks God has given us? Let us learn that wherever we're lacking, God supplies in abundance. He promised to be with Moses as he met Pharaoh, and He called on his older brother, Aaron, to help speak for him.

God pays no attention to our past or our flaws and compensates for our weaknesses when there's work to be done. He filled in Moses' gaps with His own Spirit, never failing to guide him as He'd promised. He made a reluctant Moses ready for the role of a lifetime.

Lord, here I am. Please overcome my weakness with Your strength, and let Your work begin.

REPAIR THE RIFT, WORK THE WORK

Get Mark and bring him with you, because
he is helpful to me in my ministry.
2 TIMOTHY 4:11 NIV

Paul, Barnabas, and others traveled to spread the truth, love, and grace of Jesus. In Antioch, they preached and taught, and after a while, Paul wanted them to revisit the places where they'd preached before. He and Barnabas argued sharply about Mark because he had deserted them in Pamphylia (Acts 15:36–39). Paul wanted nothing to do with him, but sometime later, things changed.

Next we know, Paul—imprisoned in Rome and not likely to be released—wanted others around him who could further the Way, and he requested Mark despite their earlier separation.

Apparently Mark recommitted himself and resumed his teaching, because even in a time of slow-moving news, Paul knew. Mark's repentance had convinced Paul of his sincerity. And as one who understood second chances well, Paul said there was no need to look back; it was time to look ahead.

It's hard to be the one welcoming back a deserter,

and it's hard to return to those we've abandoned. But Paul and Mark both realized that the work of Jesus was far more important than the flaws of the workers. Jesus knows that too and finds a way to direct us back to Him, to encourage wanderers to return to the mission.

When we get the chance, let us respond with grit to the grace given, learn from our mistakes, and make ourselves helpful in whatever ways Jesus asks.

Lord, I say yes! Please come get me and make me helpful in Your ministry.

LYING, HIDING, PRAYING, TEACHING

*"God is obviously with you, helping
you in everything you do."*
GENESIS 21:22 NLT

Before Isaac was born, Abraham lived in the foreign
and possibly hostile land of Gerar. To keep himself and
Sarah safe, he said she was his sister. So Gerar's King
Abimelech planned to take Sarah as his wife. But God
intervened and in a dream revealed to the king that
Abraham and Sarah were married.

Abimelech returned Sarah and confronted Abraham
because of the lie. "What crime have I committed
that deserves treatment like this, making me and my
kingdom guilty of this great sin? No one should ever
do what you have done!" (Genesis 20:9 NLT).

And he was right. Abraham then told the truth
(this marked the second time he had lied about Sarah),
and though Abraham had considered Gerar "a godless
place" (verse 11 NLT), God found integrity and honor
among the heathen. King Abimelech wanted to make
peace with Abraham and provided him with livestock,
servants, money, and land.

In response, Abraham prayed to God, with what I can only imagine was a good bit of gratitude, and asked for blessings for his new friend—a Philistine who heard, understood, and respected the Lord's power. God answered with healing and children for Abimelech and his people.

Only God could turn such a dangerous and delicate situation to His glory. When we're in the messes of our own making, let us too pray for God's deep intervention and resolution. Let us contribute to His work by praying for others as well.

Lord, please forgive me when
I don't trust You enough.
Know my gratitude as
others see You still helping
me in everything I do.

GRACE IN BLOOM, GROWTH IN OBEDIENCE

No discipline is enjoyable while it is happening—it's painful! But afterward there will be a peaceful harvest of right living for those who are trained in this way.

HEBREWS 12:11 NLT

Bible writers had to remind the early church of many things and encourage them through the steep learning curve on the way of Christ. The new life Jesus offered was like no other, full of freedom from arbitrary laws but equally full of obedience to God's authority. The reminder is for us all, the tender shoots of our faith reaching wild and growing best under God's governance.

If a newly planted tree, weak and untrained, is anchored down to prevent it from breaking, it grows strong. Otherwise it's pushed and pulled every which way by unfriendly winds. Without the strength to resist, it can be unrooted and die. We complain about discipline because it's never fun, but is not the sapling made stronger by the lines that hold it back?

A disciple learns the discipline of the cause he believes in. Our belief motivates us, but the practice

is not without challenge. Sometimes we fail. In His grace, Jesus doesn't give up on us; He just sturdies the lines and shows us the better way. The reining in actually helps, not hurts, and gives us power, perspective, and perseverance.

We resist correction now and then because we are who we are—human and hardheaded—but the growth that follows is worth the work. The guidance helps us overcome small errors and big issues too. Let us listen and learn because great joy is waiting for the disciplined disciple.

Lord, please help me learn from my discipline so that I rest in Your peace and grow where You've planted me.

EXPERIENCE, SHARE, REPEAT

"I cried out to the LORD in my great trouble,
and he answered me. I called to you from the
land of the dead, and LORD, you heard me!"

JONAH 2:2 NLT

It's a nice view from our high horse, isn't it? That's how Jonah felt. Secure in his religion, he tethered God to Hebrew soil and claimed redemption only for those who knew God from the beginning. He left no room for God's power or mercy to stretch beyond his own vision—a little shortsighted for a prophet.

Then God gave him a job that turned the light Jonah thought he had into the dark insides of a fish. He told Jonah to go to Nineveh, capital of Assyria and full of idol worshippers, and tell of the very grace he misunderstood. (That's one way to learn.) Jonah ran away, was swallowed by a fish then coughed up from the sea . . .and obeyed God the second time.

The Ninevites listened the first time, repented, and turned to God, who was quick to grant them grace and compassion. An angry Jonah managed to turn the unchanging character of our God into a complaint:

"I knew that you are a merciful and compassionate God, slow to get angry and filled with unfailing love" (Jonah 4:2 NLT).

Again God reminded Jonah that it was his job to act on His decisions, not make them for Him. As redeemed witnesses who know Him, that's our job too. The same grace He gave to the Ninevites is unending, and to be able to introduce others to God's grace is a job God graces us with each day. Let us complete it the first time He asks.

Lord, please fortify my belief and response when You call me to serve. Help me run to You and do Your will.

READY, SET. . .WAIT?

He said to another man, "Follow me." But he replied,
"Lord, first let me go and bury my father." Jesus
said to him, "Let the dead bury their own dead,
but you go and proclaim the kingdom of God."

LUKE 9:59–60 NIV

Jesus encountered people throughout His ministry who believed His words and wanted to be a part of all He was doing, but they sometimes questioned their place in it. They procrastinated when they had the work of the day to do and wondered how they could be broken and of benefit to Him at the same time.

He told them a life devoted to Him would require true trust and commitment, and the only cover charge was a willing heart. He didn't ask the travelers on the dusty roads of Jerusalem for a resume or a pedigree; He asked for devotion and follow-through, no matter what condition they were in. We start one place so we can finish somewhere else.

Our following encompasses our failings, so whenever we think we've put a fine enough shine on ourselves to be one of the faithful Jesus wants, we're forgetting His grace. He comes to us perfect and wants our imperfect hearts, flaws and all, and our journey together begins then and there. No waiting.

We're the Follow Jesus signs others see today, not in an "I'm better than you" way, but in the "I'm *just* like you" way. We don't have to worry about getting ready for Jesus; we just start walking where He walks because the kingdom of God is now. Ready, set, go!

Lord, I'm wounded, but I'm willing to trust You with everything I am to serve however You need. I thank You for the grace to go.

TIGHT SPOTS MAKE SPECTACULAR TESTIMONIES

But the LORD was with Joseph in the prison and showed him his faithful love. . . . The warden had no more worries, because Joseph took care of everything. The LORD was with him and caused everything he did to succeed.

GENESIS 39:21, 23 NLT

It's fun being the favorite, getting all the attention and special gifts. Joseph knew that, and maybe he enjoyed it a bit too much. His older brothers grew tired of his attitude. Out of jealousy, they actively worked to send him to a horrible life and caused almost life-ending grief for their father.

But out of Joseph's initial lack of humility and the brothers' abundance of hate, God reconciled them.

Stripped of his fancy robe, alone and deep in a pit, then captive and a slave, Joseph met others who were just as conniving as his brothers. But the horror his life had become was about to change, because somewhere along the way, he focused on his relationship with God and put that first in everything. Renewed faith and following led to new visions and victories.

In that pit or prison, betrayed or abused, we too will find a compassionate, guiding God who has not forgotten us or taken away the talents He gave us. Everything is still waiting, and the opportunity to leave our boastful ways for God's good work will arrive.

Joseph lived through fear and failure to guide nations through a famine. He came out on the other side with God not only restoring him but also granting him the power to restore his relationship with his brothers. He repaid every evil with the generosity of a redeemed soul.

Lord, please keep me mindful of Your grip that protects me in peril and guides me to represent Your grace.

REPENT, REPAIR, AND REJOICE

Weeping with joy, he embraced Benjamin, and
Benjamin did the same. Then Joseph kissed
each of his brothers and wept over them.

GENESIS 45:14–15 NLT

When we read the story of Joseph, we often focus on his life of betrayal followed by blessing as God positioned him to save millions. But his brothers experienced redemption too through the reconciliation only God could've orchestrated.

Years after Judah and the others decided to fake Joseph's death and sell him to a band of Ishmaelites, Joseph was second in command to Pharaoh and had prepared Egypt for seven years of severe famine. From everywhere, people—including Joseph's brothers— came to buy the grain only Egypt had. Joseph recognized them and sent them home with the grain they needed as well as the silver they'd brought for payment. On their second journey to buy more grain, they carried gifts and double the money, but Joseph refused payment again and filled their bags, putting his own silver cup in his younger brother Benjamin's bag. It was

a ruse that brought out the contrition and sacrifice in the brothers' hearts, and they told no lies nor tried to repeat their youthful sins. Finally Joseph could keep his secret no longer.

When he identified himself, his brothers were terrified, but that terror quickly turned to joy. In disbelief, they realized Joseph met them with forgiveness and mercy, holding no grudge and demanding no repayment: "Don't be upset, and don't be angry with yourselves for selling me to this place. It was God who sent me here ahead of you to preserve your lives" (Genesis 45:5 NLT).

Delayed change is still good change, and God sees it.

Lord, when I have a second chance, please help me respond with gratitude, humility, and love.

UNWORTHY YET CALLED, THEN AND NOW

And this time their nets were so full of fish they began to tear! . . . When Simon Peter realized what had happened, he fell to his knees before Jesus and said, "Oh, Lord, please leave me—I'm such a sinful man." . . . Jesus replied to Simon, "Don't be afraid! From now on you'll be fishing for people!"

LUKE 5:6, 8, 10 NLT

Simon Peter was a fisherman who knew frustration and doubt when everything he tried wasn't working. We know that same feeling too well, don't we? And we grow especially impatient when the failure is us.

When the catch filled the boats, Peter felt his own weakness in the face of the Savior's power. But Jesus focused not on what Peter might do wrong but on all he would do right. If at Jesus' word he could catch a load of fish without even trying, imagine what he—what we—could do with inspired determination and devotion. Following Jesus would be hard and require just that, then and now.

What we lack first in certainty Jesus graces in

confidence to move forward. Let us overcome the frustration with our world or ourselves. Jesus overcomes whatever He needs to in us when we leave everything and follow Him (Luke 5:11)—because the catch is waiting!

Everybody on the riverbank saw the miracle, and just as Jesus said, more missions and miracles would follow. Like Peter, we're human and need healing, and when Jesus steps into the boat with us, we receive His grace and guidance overflowing like the fish in those nets.

Lord, You know I'm a mess, but I'm Your mess, and I answer Your call just as I am. Please make me useful and unafraid right now.

GOD SPEAKS, WE LISTEN, HEARTS CHANGE

"I have no power to say whatever I want. I will speak only the message that God puts in my mouth."

NUMBERS 22:38 NLT

Balaam, the wicked sorcerer and worshipper of many useless gods, lived a life of magic to line his pockets with money from kings who would pay for blessings for themselves and curses for their enemies. The people of Moab were terrified of the powerful Israelites, so King Balak called on Balaam to put a curse on them. Balaam tried, but God had other plans, reaching Balaam in an amusing way: through a talking donkey. Balaam even talked back to it, perhaps appropriate for someone who spent his life calling on any name he could imagine if it helped his image and earned him money.

But eventually Balaam was convinced of the one and only God and promised no curses. Balak was undeterred and moved Balaam from place to place, as if that would make a curse stick. But each time, Balaam spoke only blessings for God's people.

When God tells us something, using any means

to get our attention, we're blessed by His mercy and guidance. When we're only adding God into the mix if it profits us, He'll take a stand and stop us too. Singular devotion to Him is the only true devotion. At first an unwilling participant, Balaam became an unstoppable witness to God's character and promise: "God is not a man, so he does not lie. He is not human, so he does not change his mind. Has he ever spoken and failed to act? Has he ever promised and not carried it through?" (Numbers 23:19 NLT).

Lord, make my allegiance
to You pure and lasting.
Please forgive and heal
my divided heart.

GO WHERE HE IS

When the Pharisee who had invited him saw this, he said to himself, "If this man were a prophet, he would know who is touching him and what kind of woman she is—that she is a sinner." . . . [Jesus said,] "I tell you, her many sins have been forgiven—as her great love has shown." . . . The other guests began to say among themselves, "Who is this who even forgives sins?"

LUKE 7:39, 47, 49 NIV

Whether Jesus was eating with them or with sinners, the Pharisees complained. But at a table ringed by those who judged so quickly, Jesus again showed the love that could right any wrong.

A woman described only as "sinful" followed Jesus there, with tears that spoke louder than any of the Pharisees' self-righteousness, and Jesus matched her love with His grace that could forgive everything. He doesn't dwell on the sin. He doesn't point out her unworthiness. He doesn't ask for payment. Instead He points out the most important feature: that she had "great love." That love called Him to her, and she went away in peace. That peace is for us too.

The woman went to Jesus and at His feet emptied everything she was. Her repentant tears opened His redemptive heart. Big brokenness requires mercy the size of which only Jesus can provide, and the result is a repair only the forgiven understand.

Let us find the courage to drop to our knees and love Him greatly so that we lead others to Him too. "Go where He is," we tell them, with the peace that we live in now. "Love Him and He will love you back even more."

Lord, when I have no words for my sin, please receive my heart and make me whole.

ONCE SURE, ALWAYS SURE

He asked for a writing tablet, and to everyone's
astonishment he wrote, "His name is John."
Immediately his mouth was opened and his tongue
set free, and he began to speak, praising God.
LUKE 1:63–64 NIV

How can I be sure? We ask ourselves that question
when we hear an unlikely prediction, especially when
it's specific to us. Gabriel arrived unexpectedly to give
Zechariah the good news of his son's upcoming birth.
It would indeed be a miracle for him and Elizabeth,
and to believe it required miraculous faith.

When Zechariah questioned the possibility of such
a blessing, Gabriel promised proof he'd not forget: "And
now you will be silent and not able to speak until the
day this happens, because you did not believe my words,
which will come true at their appointed time" (Luke
1:20 NIV).

I believe that one moment of doubt led to thousands of moments of absolute certainty for the rest of
Zechariah's life. God won't take away our promised
blessings when we hesitate for a moment, and our faith

and obedience grow as we walk in the wonder of it all. As we see everything He promises come to pass, let us praise Him too.

Let's pray for God's grace to hear and hold fast to whatever He says, without falling back into disbelief just because our limited minds struggle to understand. It's on the way—the birthing of whatever miracle we get to participate in next to glorify God. Let us call it favor and thank God for His generosity while others watch in enlightened astonishment.

Lord, I want to praise You before, during, and after any blessing You deliver. Please help me be sure about everything You say to me.

FOLLOW AND LEAD

*As he walked along, he saw Levi son of Alphaeus
sitting at his tax collector's booth. "Follow me and
be my disciple," Jesus said to him. So Levi got up
and followed him. Later, Levi invited Jesus and his
disciples to his home as dinner guests, along with
many tax collectors and other disreputable sinners.*

MARK 2:14–15 NLT

Those who considered themselves superior criticized
Jesus for eating with tax collectors and sinners. But Jesus
seems to have attracted the "scum" (Mark 2:16 NLT) with
impressive regularity. They came to Him wrecked and
broken; He welcomed them with restoration and repair.

No matter what's happened in the past, Jesus is
always focused on the future, and He not only graces
us with His mercy and forgiveness but also gifts us with
a story and influence because of it. When Jesus calls us
from a toll booth or a bed of lies or a bad attitude, it's
an opportunity to demonstrate redemption and redirection for others. The found follower is a loud follower.

Matthew (Levi) wasn't preaching against Jesus, but he
wasn't living the life God planned for him either—not

until Jesus approached him with one simple command. Matthew followed and learned to lead. He became host and helper to those just like him, and his new life was a new story he told every day. He left everything behind, finally understanding that living in the comfort he'd accepted was keeping him from living in the peaceful purpose found only in Jesus. And in some way—some miraculous, inexplicable, beyond-generous way—grace makes that new life possible for us all.

Lord, I accept Your call and follow You to tell this old story of grace made new in my life.

DOING GOD'S WORK FIRST

"From this day on I will bless you."
HAGGAI 2:19 NIV

You'd think the Israelites who returned home after years of captivity in a foreign, pagan land would've been in constant praise to their God. They were back in Judah, free, and able to complete the task of rebuilding God's house.

But they didn't build. They dawdled. They were distracted with their own houses. They felt dominated by their unfriendly neighbors. And they dared to put God off. He wanted their effort in rebuilding, but He also wanted their devotion, their remembrance of what they'd been through together and His care of them the whole way.

For twenty years, they endured drought, drawing away from God, but that was about to change. The prophet Haggai reminded them of their charge, and God would provide them a way back to Him: "This is what the LORD Almighty says: 'Give careful thought to your ways. Go up into the mountains and bring down timber and build my house, so that I may take pleasure

in it and be honored,' says the LORD" (Haggai 1:7–8 NIV).

Haggai tells us the Lord "stirred up the spirit" of all the people and they began to work (verse 14 NIV). Their chance to start over would begin with God's house, with Him at the front of their minds and their muscle.

God stands ready to stir up our spirit too when we've become distant or distracted. We can start and start over until we get it right, until we understand and embrace what comes first and build there.

Lord, thank You for the opportunity to start over when my priorities are out of order. Please keep me focused and on task.

A CALLING FORGOTTEN AND RESTORED

For we are co-workers in God's service;
you are God's field, God's building.

1 Corinthians 3:9 niv

The apostle Paul planted a church in the vital commercial city of Corinth around AD 54–55. It was an immoral place, and sadly the church shared some of its characteristics. Paul decided to write to the believers to restore balance and responsibility in the division and dysfunction there. The Christians were acting superior, as if they were somehow above the behavior Jesus asked of them. "You're better than that," Paul told them.

It's easy to become complacent, disinterested even, and just focus on the petty aggravations of the day. We forget that whatever work or worship—or battle or brawl—we participate in is an example of Christ to everyone around us. We forget that we're equipped to overcome any division among our fellow believers and any delusion that we're here for anything other than to show Jesus to others.

Paul encourages and reminds us that building up is still the goal. What we help to create is only as strong as our commitment to it, and each individual's part is crucial. What a responsibility and a privilege we have, chosen and gifted with grace to move past our mistakes and build again.

When Paul wrote to the Corinthians a second time, his affection for his fellow workers showed through. His words were "for building you up, not for tearing you down" (2 Corinthians 13:10 NIV). Jesus stands ready to help, building us up in Him. Let us serve willingly.

Lord, please forgive my pettiness and help me show that I belong to You with a reflection of Your love, generosity, and grace in everything I build.

NOT SEEING IS STILL BELIEVING

*When the Jewish Festival of Tabernacles was near,
Jesus' brothers said to him, "Leave Galilee and
go to Judea, so that your disciples there may see
the works you do. No one who wants to become
a public figure acts in secret. Since you are doing
these things, show yourself to the world." For
even his own brothers did not believe in him.*

JOHN 7:2–5 NIV

Jesus' brothers James, Joseph, Simon, and Jude had trouble believing sometimes. Fully human as they were, they wanted to see all Jesus said He could do. They wanted Him to prove with speed and flash His divinity.

"No," He said. The answer was really "not yet," and the world would just have to wait a bit. After that interchange in Galilee, Jesus taught in the temple with surprising authority. The Jews were amazed because Jesus, not being what they considered a student of the Word, really shouldn't have known all He taught. But He *was* all He taught. Soon the whole world would know too, including His young siblings. We'd all know the Jesus of miracles and Savior of souls they called *brother*.

He's here, still teaching, still the answer to every question we'll ever have. So let us do as the brothers did: stay with Him and continue to grow our faith. Let us overcome our impatience and doubts so that when we need to see Jesus move in our lives and it's taking too long, we'll remember that the answer—"not yet"—is for us too. . .and we'll believe still.

Lord, please forgive my impatience and grace me with strength to hold on to my belief as I wait for You.

IT'S GOD'S FACE
TOWARD OUR ENEMIES

"This is what the Lord says: Do not be afraid!
Don't be discouraged by this mighty army,
for the battle is not yours, but God's."
2 Chronicles 20:15 nlt

The enemy is bigger than you are. It's tough, experienced, ruthless, and headed your way. What do you do? King Jehoshaphat of Judah faced that exact situation, and understandably, he was "terrified by this news" (2 Chronicles 20:3 nlt) and worried for his people. They all began to expect a devastating future with armies coming full destruction ahead from beyond the Dead Sea. But God wouldn't leave them in their fear.

He spoke through Jahaziel, one of the priests, and told the king exactly what kind of fight was about to take place. The enemy was on its way, but the opponent waiting would be God. King Jehoshaphat traded in his unfounded fear for God's sovereign control.

God told the king not to fight but to watch in peace. And as always, God did just what He said He would—in spectacular fashion while the people praised. "At the very moment they began to sing and give praise, the LORD caused the armies of Ammon, Moab, and Mount Seir to start fighting among themselves" (verse 22 NLT).

Let's do what the king and his people did. Let's face our big and mean enemies with total confidence in God's power and might. It's hard not to be scared when we feel outmatched, but God already sees the final score. He understands our struggle and responds gloriously to our gratitude.

*Lord, my eyes are on You,
and I await Your grace
and instruction when enemies
and battles abound.*

STOP AND GO,
REDEEMED AND RECLAIMED

As they stoned him, Stephen prayed, "Lord Jesus, receive my spirit." He fell to his knees, shouting, "Lord, don't charge them with this sin!" And with that, he died. Saul was one of the witnesses, and he agreed completely with the killing of Stephen.

ACTS 7:59–8:1 NLT

Even as Saul (later known as Paul) stood by while Stephen died in testimony to God, Jesus saw far ahead. He knew Saul was holding the clothes of the murderers, enabling the horror while Stephen prayed for all of them to be saved. And He knew Saul would leave that stoning only to go "everywhere to destroy the church" (Acts 8:3 NLT). Merciless witness leads to malicious work.

Does He ever see us afraid or reluctant to take a stand, too comfortable in our own place, blind to His way? If so, our eyes are yet to be opened too.

When we don't work toward the good, we may well be fortifying the bad. By his own free admission, Paul was the worst of all of those who persecuted Christians, and we might easily say, "Well, I'm not *that* bad." What

we miss is that the future can be so much better. Even though we've failed in the past to get on the right side of things because of fear or procrastination or apathy, we're not destined to that life.

Jesus had enormous plans for Saul. And despite the horrific things he had done, promoted, or condoned, the life in front of him was full of grace to do all the remarkable things God redeemed him to do. He has enormous plans for you and me too. Let's put down the clothes and take up His cause.

Lord, replace my indifference with insight, and grace me with the courage to do what's right.

LOOK AHEAD—LET'S BUILD AND GROW

"I hid my face from you for a moment, but with everlasting kindness I will have compassion on you," says the LORD your Redeemer.
ISAIAH 54:8 NIV

Jerusalem was a mess. Facing destruction and a loss of every good thing, Isaiah delivered God's words of hope and restoration. The people had failed in their commitment to God, and their lives reflected it; but God was making great plans and wanted them to do the same.

We know the emptiness, fear, and shame too when we feel separated from God. With no one to blame but ourselves and with the haunting absence of God's gentle presence, we sit in the abyss, thinking endings instead of beginnings.

But wait. It's a temporary station. God knew then and knows now how we wander away and waste our time, and so He gives us work to build on our blessings, to fortify our future on redeemed ground. "Enlarge the place of your tent, stretch your tent curtains wide, do not hold back; lengthen your cords, strengthen your stakes" (Isaiah 54:2 NIV).

"*Prepare to grow,*" He says. "*The best is yet to be—blessings will abound!*" We have no time for fear or regret when we're looking ahead to God's promises and doing our part to receive and live the reconciled life God's grace makes possible.

The Israelites rebuilt and restored Jerusalem when they returned from their captivity in Babylon. God graces our return too. We ask for and accept God's forgiveness that's drawn in blueprint, and with trust and expectation, we build what He already sees. His compassion fuels our commitment, and the construction carries on. Let's build big!

Lord, thank You for forgiving my turning away, and bless my return with abundant growth never held back.

GET WELL AND WALK

When Jesus saw him lying there and learned that
he had been in this condition for a long time,
he asked him, "Do you want to get well?"

JOHN 5:6 NIV

The man had been at the pool in Bethesda for thirty-eight years, unable to reach the stirring waters first, as tradition said, to be healed. Then he met Jesus, who didn't care about the stirring or the water. Jesus didn't ask about the man's ailment in his legs. He focused His attention—and forced the man to focus his own—on the condition of his heart. What did he want for his life?

Jesus asks us that too, even as we sit crippled in our own procrastination, shame, lack, disbelief—anything that keeps us from getting up and following Him. But He comes to us with a plan.

He knows we can do amazing things if we'll let go of everything hurtful in our past and go forward in the profound grace He gives us every day. In whatever way we're "blind, lame, or paralyzed" (John 5:3 NLT) in our will and regardless of any excuse we come up with, Jesus gives us the same instructions He gave the

man at the pool: "Get up! Pick up your mat and walk" (verse 8 NIV).

"Get up!" *Let Me see where your heart is.*

"Pick up your mat." *Let's get to work.*

"And walk." *Keep going, don't look back. Your work lives on your will and My grace.*

The curing of the man "at once" (verse 9 NIV) is the same cure Jesus promises us if we trust our brokenness to Him. He heals us whole in His grace. Let's go.

Lord, I want to be well. I want to leave behind every hurt and go with You wherever You lead.

GOD SEES ALL, GOD OVERSEES ALL

*She gave this name to the LORD who spoke to
her: "You are the God who sees me," for she said,
"I have now seen the One who sees me."*

GENESIS 16:13 NIV

Hagar was a foreign servant to the landowner's wife,
and as was customary at the time, she was chosen to
bear Abraham a son when Sarah couldn't. The situation
wasn't easy for anyone. "When Hagar knew she was
pregnant, she began to treat her mistress, Sarai, with
contempt.... Then Sarai treated Hagar so harshly that
she finally ran away" (Genesis 16:4, 6 NLT).

Perhaps Hagar *was* smug or boastful to Sarah, and
Sarah's treatment in return was no better. We've probably been that contemptuous one before, not behaving
well in awkward circumstances, unsure what to do and
promptly doing the wrong thing. But God is always
watching. When the pregnant Hagar ran away, she ran
straight into an angel.

God saw that Hagar was afraid and insecure, and
knowing that she would find herself cast out with her
son years later (Genesis 21:8–21), He wouldn't let her

feel alone. The angel comforted Hagar and sent her back to Sarah with the grace of protection and legacy. The angel said, "I will give you more descendants than you can count. . . . You are now pregnant and will give birth to a son. You are to name him Ishmael (which means 'God hears'), for the LORD has heard your cry of distress" (Genesis 16:10–11 NLT).

We can imagine that Hagar's attitude adjustment was complete and that she would forever know that "the God who sees" was the true God of love and grace. He still is.

Lord, please keep me in gratitude, without any contempt for others, and make me obedient to Your will.

WE FOLLOW ALONE,
JOURNEY TOGETHER

Peter turned around and saw behind them the disciple
Jesus loved—the one who had leaned over to Jesus
during supper and asked, "Lord, who will betray
you?" Peter asked Jesus, "What about him, Lord?"
Jesus replied, "If I want him to remain alive until I
return, what is that to you? As for you, follow me."

JOHN 21:20–22 NLT

The world is never short of work for Jesus' followers to do, and yet we sometimes want to busy ourselves with another's responsibilities. Peter looked away from his own work to question Jesus about John's, and Jesus promptly brought his focus back to where it should be—on the path in front of him and that path alone.

"Follow Me," Jesus reminded him, and so He reminds us. It's not our place to know or intervene in another's walk with Jesus. Our own walk demands our undivided attention because it's a full-time, one-person, soul-specific job. Just like Peter, we're each uniquely designed to follow Jesus the way that best shows Him to others. And like Peter, we may forget that truth sometimes and also need a reminder.

Let us question Jesus about our journey alone. When we follow Him in the clear and precise way His grace makes possible, we discover and demonstrate our joy, purpose, and singular devotion that serves to complement the journey of the one next to us. That's how He intertwines our work with others' so that everything He's planned gets accomplished. Our job is not to intercept but to embrace.

Each of us follows alone, but together we become the swell of single-minded faith behind our Savior.

Lord, I'm grateful for my work that's special to me and gift wrapped in Your love.

FRIENDS IN UNEXPECTED PLACES

Some of the teachers of religious law who were
Pharisees jumped up and began to argue forcefully.
"We see nothing wrong with him," they shouted.
"Perhaps a spirit or an angel spoke to him." . . .
That night the Lord appeared to Paul and said,
"Be encouraged, Paul. Just as you have been
a witness to me here in Jerusalem, you must
preach the Good News in Rome as well."

ACTS 23:9, 11 NLT

Paul endured all kinds of abuse from the Pharisees because his message threatened their cushy position as leaders and teachers of the law. They held everyone accountable with no grace anywhere in their ministry. In Paul, they saw a Roman citizen who switched sides and was gaining momentum and followers with his message of undeserved grace available to everyone.

As committed as Paul was, it still would have been easy to get discouraged and tired of fighting. But Paul never gave up. God saw him doing his job well. And in a courtroom in Jerusalem, he met with some unexpected support.

On at least one occasion, the Pharisees held to the provisions and promises of God. The high council of the Sadducees condemned Paul when he talked about the resurrection of Christ. But as the authorities argued, the Pharisees defended Paul, perhaps to his surprise. Was some of his message actually getting through to the hardest hearts? Who knows? Maybe even some of those Pharisees became followers too.

God has a way of working through division and dispute to help us see what really matters. Paul's aggravation caused enough attention to have the resurrected Jesus acknowledged by unbelievers. It's a great start.

Lord, thank You for encouragement from surprising sources and the grace to continue telling others about You.

HE MADE ME DO IT

Then God looked over all he had made,
and he saw that it was very good!
GENESIS 1:31 NLT

Paradise given, paradise lost. That's the story we remember of Eve and Adam. She allowed herself to be influenced, and he followed her lead.

With all of God's very good creation before them and only one tree reserved, the first couple walked in wonder with God. They had all they needed. But the shrewd and deceitful serpent posed the fateful question to Eve that we all hear over and over: Did God *really* say that. . .and do you really believe it?

In ego, desire, and curiosity, Eve allowed herself to disobey. "She saw that the tree was beautiful and its fruit looked delicious, and she wanted the wisdom it would give her" (Genesis 3:6 NLT). No better at resisting, Adam disobeyed too, then blamed Eve. And even though He already knew, God asked, "What have you done?" (verse 13 NLT).

It's a common story. Believing the wrong people and blaming others displays our damaged humanity, but

it doesn't disqualify our original divinity. Not that we *are* God, but we are made in His unbreakable image. God works with what He has—fallen, imperfect, but devoted followers who will answer for their disobedience and carry on.

Let us listen to God's thoughts on how we're created and outfitted for this world and our work. May we then believe and obey Him in spite of all the questions we'll get from the shrewd, deceitful ones around us.

Lord, please strengthen me and help me keep my focus and faith on You when others would steer me wrong.

UNASHAMED AND EYES OPEN

At that moment their eyes were opened, and they suddenly felt shame at their nakedness. . . . "Who told you that you were naked?" the Lord God asked.

GENESIS 3:7, 11 NLT

Sometimes we don't immediately see the effects or understand the consequences of our disobedience, but Adam and Eve did. They did exactly as God told them not to do and then realized the rest of their world was changed because of it.

Originally trusting and restful in God's provision, Adam and Eve were ashamed of nothing, certainly not themselves. But then their disobedience removed their innocence, and they saw that there was evil in the world. No doubt their hearts were broken at their own evil. Suddenly alarmed at their condition, they realized they had breached the trust God put in them and had exposed their weakness. They were fearful and ashamed and wanted to cover and hide from the One who loved them most.

We know the feeling, and God's reminder is a comfort. We stand naked before Him every moment—naked

in our thoughts and faith. He sees it, good or bad, and isn't worried. But when we listen to others and allow our flaws to clothe us, we want to hide. That's when it's time to ask the revealing question: *Who's told us that we're naked?* Who's told us we're not loved by God and we're crazy to listen to Him, to trust and follow Him?

God reminds us that we—faults and all—are His, and that He's not ashamed of us. He reminded Adam and Eve of their true worth. He reminds us of that every day.

Lord, help me stand free, naked and unashamed always before You, with no need for cover, safe in Your heart.

NOW THAT'S GRACE

*For God so loved the world that he gave his
one and only Son, that whoever believes in
him shall not perish but have eternal life.*
John 3:16 niv

Jesus was never afraid of anyone or of what anyone had
done. He was far more focused on who people were
in Him—His devoted, those who said yes to "Follow
Me"—and how they would show Him to others in the
way they lived their raw, redeemed lives.

When we believe, it means we know and trust Him,
choosing His way above all others regardless of all
the ways we've gone wrong in the past. And when we
make that commitment—and then in our humanity
fail it—His never-failing grace means the promise
remains. He seeks persistent, not perfect, followers.

Jesus comes to us with that promise so that we
can go with Him to our purpose. On this journey we
travel light because He leaves all our failure and regret
in the past, relegated to a time before we claimed His
claim on us. He came here, lived this troublesome,
human life with us to know it well, and still finds some

goodness in the worst of us.

Redeemed and redirected, we have His grace to forgive the past and participate in a future full of Him. Let us learn from those flawed-yet-forgiven followers of the past who walked with Him and those we see today too, sometimes on a crooked road along with us. Our trust remains that He will not abandon us on the journey but instead accompany us to light the darkest parts.

Lord, I do believe that nothing can separate me from You. The best is yet to be because You believe in me too.

REGRET, REPENTANCE

The sacrifice you desire is a broken spirit. You will not reject a broken and repentant heart, O God.
PSALM 51:17 NLT

David went from the pasture to the palace, relying on God and obeying His commands. We know of his bravery and skill, but he was weak too.

Smitten with another man's wife, he slept with her and then set her husband up to be killed. Although his plan secured him Bathsheba, they lost their first child, and David learned the ache of total despair—afraid he had lost his God as well.

We can relate. Some transgressions are just too much for us to bear, but like David, we've not lost our God. The path forward isn't in hiding but in healing in prayer and repentance. We take responsibility for everything and then choose the only hope we have. "Create in me a pure heart, O God, and renew a steadfast spirit within me. Do not cast me from your presence or take your Holy Spirit from me" (Psalm 51:10–11 NIV).

And He listens to our prayer. There *is* life after such

a horrific lapse in judgment—and all because of His forgiveness and grace and profound love. Bathsheba "gave birth to a son, and they named him Solomon. The LORD loved him" (2 Samuel 12:24 NIV).

Regret is a powerful motivator that makes us seek God more and pray to do better. The same "Spirit of the LORD" (1 Samuel 16:13 NIV) that came on David when he was chosen never left him. We too are chosen especially for the time we're living in. Let us also chase after God's heart with all the strength we have.

Lord, please forgive me, correct me, and remind me that my heart belongs to You.

WAITING WITH GOD, WAITING FOR GOD

But do not forget this one thing, dear friends: With the Lord a day is like a thousand years, and a thousand years are like a day. The Lord is not slow in keeping his promise, as some understand slowness. Instead he is patient with you, not wanting anyone to perish, but everyone to come to repentance.

2 PETER 3:8–9 NIV

Perhaps with a little frustration, Peter pointed out to the believers in what is now Turkey and Greece that he was writing them a *second* letter to help them remember all they knew about their faith. He'd heard that they'd become a little swayed by the loud doubters of Jesus and that they'd begun to complain about waiting for Him to return and make everything better.

Maybe we've asked those same "Why not yet?" questions too, impatient and tired of defending our faith.

But this wait we're in isn't about getting to the end; it's about getting a lot more people to join us on the way. Our job here isn't to question God's timing but to show others the Jesus we know and trust, to use our faith, compassion, and wisdom to reach those lost or drowning in the pushiness of the doubters Peter talked about. Two thousand years later, they're still loud, annoying—and wrong.

Peter said to remember our learning when we're tempted to follow someone else's lead, so that we "grow in the grace and knowledge of our Lord and Savior Jesus Christ" (2 Peter 3:18 NIV). With that grace, we trust in His timing and wait with certainty and peace.

Lord, help me know what I know and learn more about You every day so I stay patient and tell others.

QUESTIONS, ANSWERS, FAITH, JOY

I will rejoice in the LORD, I will be
joyful in God my Savior.
HABAKKUK 3:18 NIV

Everything's a mess, Lord. . .and don't You care? Won't You listen? We've likely gone to God with similar complaints, wondering why He doesn't change things. He's heard it all before.

Six centuries before Christ, the prophet Habakkuk knew that God's people had failed in their faith again, and the even worse and ungodly Babylonians would be used to get them back in line. Habakkuk couldn't understand why such evil would triumph, why everyone had to suffer so much. He was angry, hurting, and confused, and after his prayers and questions, God answered. He didn't scold Habakkuk for his feelings but instead responded in quiet patience to the prophet's boldness.

That kind of dialogue is a perfect example of God's tender grace, His compassion for us when we don't understand what He's doing. Going to Him with questions means we're seeking Him, ready to listen, and

(like Habakkuk) expecting Him to answer: "I will climb up to my watchtower and stand at my guardpost. There I will wait to see what the LORD says and how he will answer my complaint" (Habakkuk 2:1 NLT).

That's the faith, persistence, attention, and interaction our Lord won't deny. He'll explain what He can and remind us to trust Him with what He won't. Habakkuk got it. No matter what was on the way, he'd look ahead—through the barren fields to a better future, secure in God's command of this world. Let us be bold too as we question in reverence and listen in faith.

Lord, thank You for listening to me at my worst and, in Your grace, reassuring me of Your presence, sovereignty, and control.

IT'S NOT THAT COMPLICATED

Don't let anyone capture you with empty philosophies and high-sounding nonsense that come from human thinking and from the spiritual powers of this world, rather than from Christ.

COLOSSIANS 2:8 NLT

Paul wrote to the followers in the small city of Colossae, worried that they were being led away from what they knew by those telling them they needed to know more. He knew the Gnostics were a threat to the young Christians. That group of teachers favored human knowledge above all else and claimed believers needed their kind of indoctrination—one dependent on self and mind, not faith and spirit—for salvation.

Paul wanted them to remember God's grace, to remember that to know Christ is not about any depth of learning or works, but purity of heart. If we begin to believe that we need something to "help" Christ along—something else to make us whole and holy—we'll forever be in futile search because the answer does not exist apart from Him. Sometimes we want to make it about us and how much we can learn and understand, but the mystery of His love and grace is to be cherished, not cataloged and categorized. We can never think or reason enough to figure it out, and we put intense pressure on ourselves to understand every facet of the Son of Man and Son of God who died and came back to life for us.

Let's not. Let's just let Him—the One who understands all—simplify it for us. Let's *follow Him*, the only philosophy we need.

Lord, help me claim the profound yet simple peace of Christ and reject anything that says it's not enough.

FIRE TEMPERED, FIRE AFLAME

*The people of the village did not welcome
Jesus. . . . When James and John saw this,
they said to Jesus, "Lord, should we call down
fire from heaven to burn them up?"*

LUKE 9:53–54 NLT

As Jesus was making His last trip to Jerusalem along with James and John, they encountered some Samaritans who didn't know or care who He was. Their disrespect led to some rash behavior by the disciples, who asked Jesus if they should call down God-given fire to punish them. Jesus said no.

While their hearts were true to Jesus, their response was way off the mark. Not only was their proposal of punishment beyond severe for the crime, but to reduce the power of God to an arbitrary tool to be summoned at will was also egotism squared.

Jesus Himself showed us how to settle disputes, how to avoid unnecessary trouble, and how to respond at the right time with all the fury of God behind us—such as when He exploded in the temple at the injustice He couldn't ignore (John 2:14–16).

And just as Jesus set the example for us, it's our responsibility to set the example for others. We can learn to assess what's happening in front of us. We can pray for guidance and discernment. And then we can respect God's authority and ability to provide justice and use us as He sees best—not the other way around.

That's what James and John did. They misjudged, Jesus set them straight, and then they continued on their way (Luke 9:56). The fire within them for God was still useful, and so is ours. Let's move.

Lord, give me the zeal of James and John and the temperance of Jesus to always respond in the way that honors You.

SURRENDER AND WIN

And yet, O Lord, you are our Father. We are the clay, and you are the potter. We all are formed by your hand. Don't be so angry with us, Lord. Please don't remember our sins forever.

ISAIAH 64:8–9 NLT

We humans can be quite the troublesome bunch for our Lord. We're so prone to forget Him, so quick to forget that His ways are best. The people of Israel, those "constant sinners" (Isaiah 64:5 NLT) just like us, had once again failed God. Isaiah pointed out a better way.

"Let God take over," he said. "Submit. Enjoy the touch of His infinite love and grace that's shown in His deep tolerance of our negligence and our need for help." We know that need, wondering if God will once again listen when we've chosen our judgment over His, when we've hurt others, been dishonest, abandoned our work, or put our trust somewhere other than the One who made us. Hmmm, maybe He won't notice?

No matter how far away we run from God, we'll never outpace Him. He's always one step ahead, too attached to us to let us out of sight.

He'll answer our call the same way He responded centuries ago, with love, patience, and the never-ending pull back to the Potter's wheel where He can mold us more, mend the breaks, and enhance the design He created in the first place. We're not tossed away; we're transformed in His loving hands. Service remains, and His grace grants our participation in it.

Lord, please help me remember my mistakes, even as You forget them, so that I gratefully surrender to Your work on me.

THE MAKING OF A MIRACLE

Another of his disciples, Andrew, Simon Peter's brother, spoke up, "Here is a boy with five small barley loaves and two small fish, but how far will they go among so many?"
JOHN 6:8–9 NIV

On the shore of the Sea of Galilee, Jesus taught more than five thousand people, and then He wanted to feed them. Philip saw the impossibility of that situation, but Andrew saw the possibility of a miracle. He brought the bread and fish to Jesus. That's our example.

Too often, we're like Philip, blind to anything we can offer Jesus. But Andrew left the decision up to Christ: "This is what we have—how far can You go with it?" And, as always, Jesus accepted what was offered to Him. He didn't complain about the condition or the presentation, didn't ask for an explanation or request more. He didn't judge; He blessed.

Yet we worry that our offering today will be received some other way, that what we bring to Him is too deficient, too damaged to be part of anything. So He asks *us* a question: What now? It's our own exercise in loaves and fishes—where the miracle of our life isn't the result of what we have but what He does with it.

When we surrender to Jesus what we are and whatever we've done, He'll multiply it to be more than enough and make a miracle out of it for us too. What we give to Jesus becomes more than it was in order to accomplish all that He wants. Let the multiplication begin.

Lord, please take all I have to give and make me all You want me to be.

OBEY ONCE, OBEY ALWAYS

Then Samson prayed to the LORD,
"Sovereign LORD, remember me. Please,
God, strengthen me just once more."
JUDGES 16:28 NIV

God created Samson, the boy with superior strength and rules to follow, to "take the lead in delivering Israel from the hands of the Philistines" (Judges 13:5 NIV). And while Samson followed God's guidelines in many ways, including never cutting his hair, he was impulsive and lustful, and his dalliance with Delilah cost him his greatest gift.

Samson may have been in love, but Delilah sold him out to his old enemies, the Philistines. With arms tied, eyes gouged, and head shaved, Samson was put to work in prison. Sometimes we've taken great strength in whatever form God gave it and traded it away foolishly too, finding ourselves imprisoned in our own regret and unable to see a way out.

But God always has a contingency plan, and His will cannot be overthrown by our poor judgment. Samson was blind and shackled, "but the hair on his

head began to grow again" (Judges 16:22 NIV). While the Philistines celebrated and praised their worthless god Dagon, God graced Samson with power to destroy thousands of them and their temple, fostering the separation of His people from the pagans. Samson became a casualty of war, but he completed his task as a deliverer of God's judgment.

God won't abandon us even when we make fulfilling our mission harder, and He'll strengthen us too when we pray, "O Sovereign Lord. . . ." Let us always return when we've strayed. God will meet us there.

Lord, please find the goodness in me when I fail, and strengthen me to carry out Your will.

FOCUS, FAITH, AND FOLLOW-THROUGH

So let's not get tired of doing what is good. At just the right time we will reap a harvest of blessing if we don't give up.
GALATIANS 6:9 NLT

The Christians of the Roman province of Galatia were not Jews. They were followers organized and taught by Paul and Barnabas, and they were taught that Jesus is our Savior by our faith in Him, not our reliance on a rule book.

But Jews in the area focused on keeping all the laws of Moses in order for salvation to stick, and this teaching was weakening the Galatians' faith and fortitude. They were confused and in need of clarification and courage.

Sometimes we are too. If we begin to think our faith depends on anything other than the grace of God and our resurrected Savior, we feel unable to keep sowing for the harvest. If we let any requirement lead us other than loving God and loving others—the two greatest commandments on which Jesus hung every law (Matthew 22:36–40)—then we'll be overwhelmed and likely fall away. We'll see no hope of being the Christian we want

to be, of "doing what is good."

But that hope is what Jesus made possible and Paul made simple: follow Jesus and do what He tells us. In His grace we are saved, and in His grace we go forward. Our part is to not give up, to keep going despite what nonbelievers might say. Then we'll finish sowing, reap the harvest, and then sow some more. We gather because Jesus planted us here. Grace begets grace.

Lord, please help me focus on the work of loving You and loving others, no rules needed.

GOD WATCHES, GOD WAITS

*"Why are you so angry?" the Lord asked
Cain. "Why do you look so dejected? You will
be accepted if you do what is right. But if you
refuse to do what is right, then watch out!"*
Genesis 4:6–7 nlt

When the first two brothers brought their sacrifices
before the Lord, only one lived to tell about it. Abel,
the rancher with a pure heart, brought the firstborn
of his flock, and God was pleased. Cain, the farmer
with less than pure intentions, brought what he raised,
but it found no favor with God. Cain responded with
anger—anger that God told him to control before it
controlled him. Cain killed his brother and lost his
place in God's Eden, becoming a "homeless wanderer"
(Genesis 4:12 nlt).

When we commit evil acts, we feel the same despair,
knowing we've failed God and caused unspeakable pain
to others. How can we recover, and can God's grace be
strong enough for what we've done?

The only sacrifice God wanted was the devotion of
a sincere heart. In fear and submission, Cain realized

that what he wanted was not to be separated from God. "My punishment is too great for me to bear! You have banished me from the land and from your presence" (verses 13–14 NLT).

God's compassion and mercy persisted, and He "put a mark on Cain to warn anyone who might try to kill him" (verse 15 NLT). Cain was separated from all he knew, but God was watching. Perhaps they reconciled and Cain rebuilt his life on renewed faith and sincere devotion. We know that's what we'd pray for.

Lord, some sins are too big for me to carry, and I can only leave them with You and seek restoration in Your grace.

FINDING JESUS

Three days later they finally discovered him in the
Temple. . . . All who heard him were amazed at his
understanding and his answers. His parents didn't
know what to think. "Son," his mother said to him,
"why have you done this to us? Your father and I
have been frantic, searching for you everywhere."

LUKE 2:46–48 NLT

What? Joseph and Mary lost Jesus?

On their way home to Nazareth after the Passover festival in Jerusalem, Mary and Joseph were in a panic, unable to find Jesus. They turned around and three days later found the twelve-year-old still in Jerusalem. He was in the temple, teaching and learning.

Maybe that's what we need to do too when we feel we've lost Jesus—turn around and go back to our purest worship of our Savior, listening and learning as He teaches from His heart all we need to know.

That's what Jesus told His parents—it should've been an easy search because they should've known that He "must be in [His] Father's house" (Luke 2:49 NLT). Let us be grateful for whatever drives us back in search of Jesus.

We can never really lose Him, though, because He won't lose us. He's tethered to us by the greatest love in all the known and unknown universe. Whether apart for three minutes or three decades, we return to the special place He holds for us in His heart. That moment of horrifying panic when we think He's missing might feel as long as a three-day donkey ride in the desert, but it's one breath away from resting in His inconcealable grace.

Lord, please find me
quickly when I lose You
. . .and teach me too.

FINDING JESUS AGAIN

The Jewish leaders demanded, "What are
you doing? If God gave you authority to do
this, show us a miraculous sign to prove it."
"All right," Jesus replied. "Destroy this temple,
and in three days I will raise it up."
JOHN 2:18–19 NLT

Jesus was lost from His parents and taught at the temple in Jerusalem when He was twelve. He returned twenty years later to clear the temple of the blasphemy and unbelievers and to make a promise almost no one would believe.

The Jews who listened to Jesus were always looking for anything to throw Him off, often demanding miracles to prove His authority. Jesus' enigmatic answer of raising the temple in three days was meant for His disciples and proven to them with the sunrise of Easter morning. If anyone was doubtful about the way, He laid out the road map to guide them forever.

It was a hard time to be a believer, and perhaps the disciples had their own questions and limited understanding when Jesus spoke these words. After the resurrection, though, they remembered His words and taught with greater authority because He'd prepared them for all their work to come.

Jesus does that for us too. Maybe in a way that we'll not understand until later, He shows us a truth or reassurance or reminder that He is who He said He is. And no matter what, we find Him again when we seek to know Him better. We often think too small. Let's think resurrection-size grace that no one can miss.

Lord, please always lead me to You on the path I know best, the path paved with Your love and grace.

BOUNDARIES BREACHED, MISSIONS REMAIN

*Look to the LORD and his strength;
seek his face always.*
1 CHRONICLES 16:11 NIV

Before Solomon asked God for a discerning heart, he "showed his love for the LORD" (1 Kings 3:3 NIV). That was already wise. God was pleased with Solomon's request for wisdom and responded with riches and honor as well. *"But stay obedient,"* God advised. And for the most part, Solomon did, meting out justice, reigning in peace, providing for his people, and building the first temple for God in a thousand years.

Solomon's reach and his power were great, and when the whole world seems to belong to you, it can be hard to resist anything. God asked again for "integrity of heart and uprightness" (1 Kings 9:4 NIV). It was not an idle request.

"King Solomon, however, loved many foreign women" (1 Kings 11:1 NIV), and that indulgence led to favoring their pagan gods as well. Perhaps that's the lesson and something we've seen in ourselves too. When

we lose "integrity of heart" in one boundary, it's easier to allow a crack in another.

But God puts no expiration date on His gifts, and we shouldn't either. Solomon sought forgiveness as well as wisdom to keep doing his job. "Do not neglect your gift," Paul told us a millennium later (1 Timothy 4:14 NIV). What we receive from God is meant to be used by us, the imperfect souls who house it.

All of us would do well to remember the words of Solomon's father, David, to seek God's face always. If we're looking at Him, we'll see reflected back the wisdom and strength to follow His will.

Lord, help me keep integrity of heart in everything I do. Forgive my disobedience and use me still.

DRAW YOUR DECREE
AND SET YOUR STONE

"If you refuse to serve the LORD, then choose today whom you will serve. . . . But as for me and my family, we will serve the LORD."

JOSHUA 24:15 NLT

Despite the miraculous care, unparalleled victories, and continuous grace God had delivered to the Israelites through Abraham, Moses, and others, the Israelites wanted to worship man-made idols and far-fetched beings they thought might just give them something they desired.

It's easy to condemn them. It's easy to be them. We too can forget where everything good comes from and focus on what everything else promises. Money, fame, security, power, acquisition, glory—these idols tempt us every day and in every way. And the time comes when we have to choose, when we humble ourselves, return to God, and receive His grace to carry on, wiser and still undeniably loved.

Joshua told the people they needed to choose either the Almighty God or the worthless gods. They chose well. "The people said to Joshua, 'We will serve the LORD our God. We will obey him alone'" (Joshua 24:24 NLT).

To commemorate their obedience and renewed commitment, Joshua made a covenant for the people and set a large stone where they worshipped God to be a witness to their continued allegiance. I'll set my stone too, in front of my heart, and return to my God, who never left my side. He waited for me so that now I can wait for His instruction. I'm still His.

Lord, clear my thoughts and deeds of anything I think is more powerful or desirable than You. Keep me true.

BENT IN SHAME, SENT IN SERVICE

Jesus returned to the Mount of Olives, but early the next morning he was back again at the Temple. A crowd soon gathered, and he sat down and taught them. As he was speaking, the teachers of religious law and the Pharisees brought a woman who had been caught in the act of adultery. They put her in front of the crowd.

JOHN 8:1–3 NLT

Here were the teachers again, trying to catch Jesus in a situation He couldn't figure out. They pulled a woman from an adulterous bed into the temple square and demanded, "The law of Moses says to stone her. What do you say?" (John 8:5 NLT).

The woman knew that if she were caught, she'd be shamed and killed in front of everyone, by everyone. There was no hope of mercy or forgiveness as she lay in a heap on the ground. She saw Jesus as just another person to tower over her and condemn her. But instead she met the Jesus who bent down to console her and, in His grace, give her new life.

No one stepped forward to throw a stone, and as the

crowd slipped away, perhaps Jesus' grace showed them their hypocrisy, giving them a chance to change too. That's the point Jesus makes so clearly to us all. "'Then neither do I condemn you,' Jesus declared. 'Go now and leave your life of sin'" (John 8:11 NIV). He urges us to receive the mercy He stoops to pour on our broken spirits, to go forward *His* way, away from whatever's leading us awry.

For you and me too, the failure lies on the ground; the future lives in His grace.

Lord, thank You for Your grace that changes my life and bears witness to others. Let us all go wherever You say.

STARTING SOMEWHERE

John said to Jesus, "Teacher, we saw someone using
your name to cast out demons, but we told him
to stop because he wasn't in our group." "Don't
stop him!" Jesus said. "No one who performs a
miracle in my name will soon be able to speak evil
of me. Anyone who is not against us is for us."
MARK 9:38–40 NLT

Don't we all love a backstage pass, relish belonging
to our group, and like to keep our privileged powers
to ourselves? When the disciples saw people who weren't
one of them speaking for Jesus, they were quick to
judge. They saw actions that demonstrated a love of
Christ, but they decided that wasn't enough to welcome the outsiders to the Lord of lords. The benevolent
anarchy must be stopped, they decided. Jesus saw something else.

The disciples had a priceless opportunity to teach
more about Christ—the most inclusive Being of love
ever—but perhaps they had elevated themselves from
a time of simple faith and basic acts to policing the
masses. "Return to the simple splendor of water for a

thirsty brother," Jesus told them.

Maybe we've also sat in judgment, or maybe we've been the unschooled but hungry-for-more soul with a heart in the right place. Our awareness of "something" behind what we do is the first step toward the incorporation of Christ in everything we do. Let us not be afraid to step out or gather in. If you're for me, I'm for you, and we're both for Jesus. That's good enough.

Lord, help me give and receive anything that helps another in Your name. You'll decide what comes next.

SHARE THE BURDEN, SHARE THE TRIUMPH

"This job is too heavy a burden for you to handle all by yourself. Now listen to me, and let me give you a word of advice, and may God be with you."

Exodus 18:18–19 NLT

Sometime while Moses guided the Israelites on their journey to Canaan, he had sent his wife and sons to stay with her father, Jethro, in Midian. To reunite the family, Jethro brought Moses' wife and the boys back to him as he "camped near the mountain of God" (Exodus 18:5 NLT), where Moses was at work.

Moses had done amazing things—leading the Israelites out of bondage, intervening between the people and God, and speaking for the Lord. Then he continued to serve as judge—mediating every dispute, praying for insight, and relaying God's response. It was noble but exhausting work, and Jethro recognized the problem right away. Even better, he offered a solution. Jethro told Moses to continue teaching God's decrees—in other words, to do what he did best—and to recruit others who were capable and honest to help

with day-to-day matters. "If you follow this advice," Jethro said, "and if God commands you to do so, then you will be able to endure the pressures" (verse 23 NLT).

We can put a similar burden on ourselves and try to do everything for everyone, perhaps forgetting our greatest gifts in the process too. Let us pray for wise friends who see and advise, "Listen to me, but ask God about what I say."

Moses humbled himself to Jethro's advice, just in time. He was about to ascend that "mountain of God" and receive His commandments.

Lord, help me see when I need to adjust my work and heed good advice from those who love and trust You.

BE CAREFUL WHAT YOU LAUGH AT

Then the LORD said to Abraham, "Why did
Sarah laugh? Why did she say, 'Can an old
woman like me have a baby?' Is anything too
hard for the LORD? I will return about this
time next year, and Sarah will have a son."

GENESIS 18:13–14 NLT

Sometimes in the quiet, deep of our souls, we hear a promise from God. It seems impossible, so we laugh about it, nervous and unsure. Is it because we doubt God, we doubt ourselves, or we doubt we heard the promise at all? In any case, we dismiss God's words. We shake our heads at the possibility of the promise. How could it be? Maybe we're just tired because hope carried too long becomes heavy. It's easier to deny than to dream on. Sarah did that.

After years with no child and after contriving the birth of another, she didn't dare believe God was about to grant her aging request. But God hears, forgives, and answers prayers, delighting us and serving His own grand purposes at the same time, at the right time. Whether it's a promise or a reassurance or a challenge,

when God makes up His mind to fill us up, it's so we can empty ourselves onto others.

Out of Sarah's barrenness came the beginning of the nation of Israel. God blessed Sarah with good health, the ability to deliver a healthy baby, and the strength to raise him up in a challenging world. Her doubt and despair displayed as laughter led to the life of motherhood she longed for and lived out, forever impacting our own.

God still uses salvaged faith to save His world.

Lord, please help me respond to Your promises with joy, confidence, and commitment as I wait to see what You see.

BEING LEAST

His disciples began arguing about which of them was the greatest. But Jesus knew their thoughts, so he brought a little child to his side. Then he said to them, "Anyone who welcomes a little child like this on my behalf welcomes me, and anyone who welcomes me also welcomes my Father who sent me. Whoever is the least among you is the greatest."

LUKE 9:46–48 NLT

What did Jesus mean when He elevated the "least" to the "greatest"? It goes against our self-centered logic where "great" means records and accolades, admiration and recognition from the masses. But Jesus saw it differently. The greatest isn't the one who knows the most or achieves the most but the one who is completely surrendered to Jesus, welcoming His direction with the faith of a trusting child. The only way to do more is to have more of Jesus.

The disciples knew that they had lots of important work to do and that it would require all their talent, skill, and tenacity. So do we, and we want to do it all right, do it all well. But we do it all best when we work

in the background, believing that Jesus takes our effort and makes it worthwhile.

Let's not worry about who is watching besides Jesus. To all the others, let's simply demonstrate Him, up close and personal, the way a little one wants to hold your face when you talk to him. What matters is the message, and our humble focus shouts the greatest news in all the world.

Lord, I'm greatest when I'm least, when I'm open, receptive and reflective of You. Please help me remember that every day.

ONLY ONE QUESTION MATTERS

"Listen now, and I will speak; I will
question you, and you shall answer me."
JOB 42:4 NIV

The "patience of Job" is legendary and elusive. None of us want to go through what he did, and when we're enduring times of loss or pain or confusion, we're tempted to be more like Job's mouthy friends than the enlightened servant, Job himself.

Job's suffering was a horrific loss and surprise, and no one expected to see "the greatest man among all the people of the East" (Job 1:3 NIV) stripped of land, livestock, and loved ones. He refused to blame God through it all, even when his body was attacked as well. Then a few friends stopped by with the comfort of a hurricane.

Job continued to defend God, but the test was hard. He began to wonder if God was mad at him, had deserted him. He cried out in despair, demanding answers he had no right to request. It's God's place to ask and direct, ours to answer and follow.

Like Job, we learn we only need to ask God one question: "What's next, Lord?" That's the question asked

in hope and humility that will be answered in grace and guidance because God is God through loss and longing, redemption and recovery.

And one of Job's next tasks was to reflect some of God's grace onto those "miserable comforters" (Job 16:2 NIV) who failed him. It's never wrong to respond with kindness. "After Job had prayed for his friends, the LORD restored his fortunes and gave him twice as much as he had before" (Job 42:10 NIV), including 140 more years of service to his God.

Lord, help me stand firm in loss and focus on You, willing and able to take the next step You order.

GRACE ALL AROUND

"Let's have a feast and celebrate. For this son of mine was dead and is alive again; he was lost and is found."
LUKE 15:23–24 NIV

In the story of the prodigal son, the lost-and-found beloved, we see an example of Jesus' grace in all its purity and truth. If we've been that wayward, arrogant child welcomed home, we know that kind of love. If we're still working our way back, let us hurry and accept the gift of His grace, because a pigpen is no place for a child of the living God.

We're found to work, not wallow in our own self-pity or shame. That lost son had amends to make, and he was equipped to do that because he was made whole by the unconditional love of his father. He was redeemed so we could see. Alive again, his past remained, but the future was more important because God doesn't have a rear-view mirror.

The brother at home needed a redirection too. He was offended and petulant, jealous and hurt, and we've reacted the same way when we're focused more on the before than the after and more on judgment than mercy. That's a need for grace too. As his father told him, we all participate in the celebration when the lost are found.

God's grace covers those who return from faraway and those with hard hearts. He brings all closer to Him so that our lives are proof of the inexplicable love of an incomprehensible Savior who welcomes us back to send us forth. The returning is only the beginning.

Lord, thank You for calling me worthy, even though I've failed You so. Please take this broken life You've made whole and put me to work.

OBEDIENCE EVERYWHERE, VICTORY EVERYWHERE

"Now come with me, and see how devoted I am to the LORD."
2 KINGS 10:16 NLT

Jehu was a fierce military leader as the Israelite nation was spreading and gaining ground. God told Elisha to anoint Jehu king, and Jehu immediately got to work. We do that too—so proud of our calling, so obedient to our God. Until we're not.

Jehu was especially offended by witchcraft and idolatry, and he destroyed the bad seeds from the house of Ahab and others. He also deceived the ministers of Baal, the Canaanite god, and killed them all. Then he turned their temple into a bathroom.

To rid the Israelite land of pagan worship was God's plan, and Jehu did almost everything as ordered; but he chose to let the golden calves at Bethel and Dan remain, sort of a conciliatory gesture to political rivals-turned-subjects.

Jehu's way of trying to keep a bit of control, just in case God wasn't in complete control of the situation,

was a lack of loyalty and trust. But God worked around Jehu's weak spots to create a better, purer life for His people because He won't throw away all the good we've done when we make a mistake.

Let us learn from Jehu that we truly obey God when we obey everything He says. Our way isn't going to be best if it's outside His directive. To participate with God in making the world a better place is to live in the grace of the Master of all plans. Let's do our part and trust Him with the rest.

Lord, help me listen only and completely to You. Help me challenge every other thought and test it against Your instruction.

SABBATH MADE FOR MAN

"Now if a boy can be circumcised on the Sabbath
so that the law of Moses may not be broken,
why are you angry with me for healing a man's
whole body on the Sabbath? Stop judging by mere
appearances, but instead judge correctly."

JOHN 7:23–24 NIV

When Jesus dared heal a lame man on the Sabbath, the
legalists eagerly called Him on it, pouncing on a *gotcha*
moment they hoped to use to discredit Jesus and His
teaching. They were wrong.

His answer quieted them and passed a serving of
grace to us, showing us that if we obsess over one bent
rule, we might miss the bigger "save" God has planned
for us. Just as Jesus focused on the more important
need in front of Him, so can we.

It's about distilling the whole situation and choosing
the correct—if sometimes nonconforming—action that
makes something better, the brave action that shows
Jesus to someone who needs Him. In any exchange
that focuses on Him, we are forever blessed.

Let us learn from the persnickety Pharisees and look

past the trees of legalism to the forest of love, reaching out and risking a step aside to step forward the same way Jesus did. God's grace gives us the wisdom to recognize those times and the courage to live well in them.

And let us see healing for ourselves in a less complicated way too. God heals us when we humbly ask, and that healing makes us whole to help others see that God's healing is bound by no law and hindered by no rule. His grace *is* the rule.

Lord, please help me see the landscape You see and walk only in obedience to You.

STOP. GO FORWARD.

Listen! The LORD's arm is not too weak to save you, nor is his ear too deaf to hear you call. It's your sins that have cut you off from God. Because of your sins, he has turned away and will not listen anymore.

ISAIAH 59:1–2 NLT

Isaiah had a long list of the Israelites' sins he could preach about. Our sins, large or small, separate us from God just as Israel's sins separated them from God. If we want His grace and forgiveness, do we ask with a pure and repentant heart?

At this time, the people who claimed to love and serve God were guilty of injustice, hostility, rebellion, treachery, and forsaking everything God meant to them. Their hands were "stained with blood," literally (Isaiah 59:3 NIV), with other sins on top. We only make matters worse when we're going the wrong way and can't hear God's voice. But He hears us.

God forgives and guides us back to Him, the only place from which we can do anything. And He would no sooner turn His back on us than on the whole nation of Israel. So we see the present for what it is, thank

God the past is in the past, and ask Him to walk into the future with us.

God's Spirit is always responsive, and no price He pays is too high for the value He sees in us. "'The Redeemer will come to Jerusalem to buy back those in Israel who have turned from their sins,' says the LORD" (verse 20 NLT). Let us practice repentance too and redeploy our lives in the grace God gives to reveal His glory.

Lord, thank You for Your arms that pull me back to You when I turn away. Let's go forward together.

IT'S NEVER TOO LATE
TO BE AN EXAMPLE

Then he said, "Jesus, remember me when you come
into your Kingdom." And Jesus replied, "I assure
you, today you will be with me in paradise."
LUKE 23:42–43 NLT

Of the two guilty, desperate men flanking Jesus on the
hilltop of Calvary, only one of them died in his sin.
The other man is sometimes called a thief, sometimes
a murderer. Regardless of what brought him to that
cross, he understood the idea of mercy and the power
of redemption. With grace he couldn't grasp, he realized that the Son of Man next to him could right all the
wrong he'd ever done.

The man was brave and repentant enough to ask
for Jesus' forgiveness, and even at the point of His own
natural death, Jesus focused on the immediate need.
With the whispers of His last breath, He saved one
we might call undeserving. He asked His followers to
reach out, witness, and grow the church, but He knew
this man could do nothing to help anyone. Then again,
maybe he does.

As Jesus promised, the man went to paradise that day, and his life and death remind us today that Jesus is forever able and willing to answer our pleas too. That same precious grace is offered to all of us, and we're still here to reflect it to everyone who will listen and watch. Every extension of His grace demonstrates its infinite, overarching power—available to us all, no matter how we wind up on that cross. If we're beside Jesus, we're in the place where everything is possible.

Lord, please forgive me and remember me. Help me use whatever time I have to show Your grace to others.

RIVALRY, REASSESSMENT, AND RESPECT

The boundary lines have fallen for me in pleasant places; surely I have a delightful inheritance.
PSALM 16:6 NIV

Jacob was in love with Rachel. He worked seven years for her father so he could marry her. Then after being tricked into marrying her older sister, Leah, he worked seven more years for Rachel. And so began a long story of anger and resentment, testing and trickery.

Leah knew Jacob loved Rachel more, and barren Rachel was jealous of Leah's children. They each fought and connived to get what they wanted, perhaps their years growing up together making things worse.

We can behave just like the sisters—jealous of others' blessings or success—especially when we feel rejected or inadequate ourselves. But God thinks in terms of abundance, not acrimony. *"Grow where you are,"* He says. There's no shame in anything He's given or withheld.

We know that Jacob never abandoned either sister, and they both raised sons crucial to Israel's history, dearly loved and honored. Whatever someone else has

or does is no reflection on the beauty of the gifts and the depth of the promises God gives us. Any need to "win" blinds us to the good. We can do better. We can replace competition with collaboration, rivalry with rallying those around us to do better too.

Yes, it's a big, challenging task to overcome our sadness and disappointment to celebrate with another, but it's right. God has put our boundary lines in place for a good reason, and when we work and worship where we are, others see God in everything we do.

Lord, help me cheer others on, see You in their lives, and reflect You in mine.

COURAGE TO GO BACK,
COURAGE TO GO FORWARD

He is very dear to me but even dearer to you, both
as a fellow man and as a brother in the Lord.
PHILEMON 16 NIV

We've all been there—wanting to run from our past—but
we can only overcome our past when we run back to it
and tell it goodbye. We're weak and empty, but God fills
us with His grace so we can go forward to a better life.

In just twenty-five verses, Paul asked one brother
in Christ to return, repent, and reconcile and the
other brother to extend grace as exemplified by Christ
Himself. Onesimus was a slave for the wealthy Colossian
Philemon, but he'd run away, perhaps for stealing (verse
18). Somewhere along the line, he encountered Paul
and found Jesus.

Instead of keeping Onesimus with him, Paul encouraged him to return to Philemon and ask forgiveness,
knowing how hard that would be. Paul also wrote to
Philemon to explain this request. Appealing to their
shared salvation, Paul asked Philemon to pass on the
grace none of us deserve to the guilty Onesimus, even

offering to repay anything Onesimus owed.

As guilty as Onesimus was and we've been, the only way we can hope to do anything is to return to Christ, repent for what we've done wrong, and receive the reconciliation He offers in the grace that covers everything. Let's be sure that we run to the only One who can put us back to work doing what only we can do. A restored relationship with Him is the reason He came. Let's not waste it.

Lord, make me brave enough to admit my dependency on You for the grace to start over.

DON'T GIVE UP—GET UP AND DANCE

For his anger lasts only a moment, but his favor lasts a lifetime; weeping may stay for the night, but rejoicing comes in the morning.
PSALM 30:5 NIV

We have so many challenging and consoling words from David the shepherd king, as if he were in constant prayer and petition with God. And maybe he was as he searched his heart and turned to God in every circumstance of his life.

He failed, miserably and publicly at times, but he continued to trust in God's ability and willingness to forgive him, teach him, and restore him. We all fail and hurt too when we've disappointed God or disobeyed His instructions.

But confident to his core in God's love, David went unafraid to Him more than once to ask for attention and help. He stood ready to learn from his mistakes and carry on better and wiser because he knew nothing good would come from just giving up. "What is gained if I am silenced, if I go down to the pit? Will the dust praise you? Will it proclaim your faithfulness?

Hear, LORD, and be merciful to me; LORD, be my help" (Psalm 30:9–10 NIV).

And in the next breath, David was dancing instead of wailing (verse 11). That's the picture of a soul redeemed, restored, and ready to try again, ready to sing about the grace that comes only from God and be witness to others of its power. Not perfect but perfectly dependent on Him—that's right where He wants us.

Lord, I come to You in pain, and I trust Your grace to repair and prepare me for all that's to come. Let others see what You can do.

EVERYBODY'S WATCHING

But when Peter came to Antioch, I had to oppose him to his face, for what he did was very wrong. When he first arrived, he ate with the Gentile believers, who were not circumcised. But afterward, when some friends of James came, Peter wouldn't eat with the Gentiles anymore. He was afraid of criticism from these people who insisted on the necessity of circumcision. As a result, other Jewish believers followed Peter's hypocrisy, and even Barnabas was led astray by their hypocrisy.
GALATIANS 2:11–13 NLT

Peter had learned from Jesus that the old laws gave way to the new grace He provided, and yet he returned to the law when it suited him. It was an ironic turn with a case of whiplash. The Jesus that Peter followed taught about accepting everyone and judging no one, and the Peter that the new believers followed left those believers because he was afraid of being unaccepted and judged by others who followed the Jesus who taught about accepting everyone and judging no one. It makes me dizzy.

Paul called Peter out on his behavior toward the Gentiles and took the opportunity to remind us that it's our faith that Jesus cares about, and no rule we add or take away can make Him love us any more or less. "And we have believed in Christ Jesus, so that we might be made right with God because of our faith in Christ, not because we have obeyed the law. For no one will ever be made right with God by obeying the law" (Galatians 2:16 NLT).

The grace of Christ painted on us means we're the picture of Christ to everyone. Let Him shine through.

Lord, please help me be Your arms and Your heart that welcome those who seek You.

GOD COUNTS US ENOUGH

*"O Sovereign LORD," I said, "I can't
speak for you! I'm too young!"*
JEREMIAH 1:6 NLT

Young Jeremiah lived in a time of war, defeat, rebellion, and captivity. It's no wonder he questioned his own God-given abilities. What could he possibly contribute to help the people in peril around him?

We feel unworthy and useless too sometimes, and no one likes to be the bearer of bad news, but hope and redemption are coming—are *always* coming when God has a message for those He loves. Jeremiah fortified himself with that knowledge, did his job, and focused on the promise he trusted God to fulfill. He was perfectly able and graced for the task.

It's easy to dismiss urgings from God, to ignore a mission that surely couldn't have been designed for us. Who do we think we are anyway? We're only believers, not Bible scholars. We're only learners, not teachers. We're only sinners, not saints. But God is older than time and Seer of all. Our condition is a variable, not a deal breaker. Age, color, size, gender. It doesn't matter to God, because we are never "only" anything or "too" anything. Grace finds a way when God has set the path.

But if we don't obey God's instructions, our work can go undone. If we lack confidence, certainty, or courage, we'll doubt our abilities and get stymied before we even begin. I'm only one person, but God speaks to one person at a time. God says I'm His alone, too precious to abandon. He claims me, and that's enough. His grace makes me enough.

Lord, You know my insecurities well. Please guide me with Your grace and help me put my doubts away and get to work.

JUST KEEP SHOWING EVERYONE WHO'LL LISTEN

One night the Lord spoke to Paul in a vision and told him, "Don't be afraid! Speak out! Don't be silent! For I am with you, and no one will attack and harm you, for many people in this city belong to me."

ACTS 18:9–10 NLT

In Corinth, the Jews opposed and abused Paul so much that he was ready to abandon them and go to the Gentiles. We know he moved on to that part of his ministry eventually, but first he had more to say where he was. As instructed, he kept "teaching the word of God" (Acts 18:11 NLT).

It's hard to teach a way of life based on love, forgiveness, faith, and grace in the face of opposition based on protocol, pedantry, doctrine, and legalism. But Paul kept going, kept teaching. For another eighteen months he probably explained the same gift of new life in Christ a million times. Many believed, and no doubt his extra time with Aquila and Priscilla helped them become the leaders they were.

Together they all kept the faith and taught whoever

would listen. They answered every argument with the truth of Jesus and an invitation to join them at His feet, where they found real grace to leave everything hurtful behind and watch their world change. Paul, Aquila, and Priscilla lived what they taught, being graced themselves to show that grace to others.

Even if our audience today is stubborn, reluctant, or uninterested, we don't fail if we live what we teach, daily calling on God's grace to keep changing our world too. To keep quiet is the real loss.

Lord, please help me be a witness to You wherever I am, unafraid to speak out, and live out what it means to follow You.

NOT TOO GOOD TO BE TRUE

*"Now I know that there is no God
in all the world except in Israel."*
2 Kings 5:15 nlt

Naaman was a great military commander for the king of Aram near Israel, but he was no follower of God. When a young Israelite girl who worked for Naaman's wife saw his leprosy, she displayed her own faith and encouraged him to see the prophet Elisha. Elisha told Naaman to wash seven times in the Jordan River, and Naaman pretty much equated that with stepping in a mud puddle, which he could've done at home, and in better waters (verse 12). Sometimes we just don't want to look foolish. But convinced by his officers, he followed Elisha's advice—and soon became a believer, made whole inside and out. He was healed and awakened at the same time.

Naaman didn't know about God's grace before, and he expected a far more challenging task in order to be cured. He was focused on the act of the body, not the condition of the heart. The seven washes in the water surely seemed arbitrary and trivial, but he was being asked to have faith in the one true God.

God's grace is given in response to our acceptance and faith, and the trust demonstrated in the smallest act fills His heart with affection for us. I can see Him smiling back at us when we receive something so grand for what we consider so little and realize there is no end to His desire to give, nothing better than our love and devotion in return.

Lord, help me put my faith before my actions and trust the grace that comes from Your pure and generous heart.

NOT ME. . .YES, ME

And immediately the rooster crowed the second time. Suddenly, Jesus' words flashed through Peter's mind: "Before the rooster crows twice, you will deny three times that you even know me." And he broke down and wept.

MARK 14:72 NLT

How could he? We might have thought Peter, full of fire and faith, could never fail to claim Jesus as his own. He was willing to draw his sword, after all, but then he stumbled in drawing a line between himself and nonbelievers. Why?

Jesus predicted the three denials of Peter, and of course Peter said he'd die before disowning Him. This story of recovery is important enough for all four Gospel writers to tell us about it. And it's the story of us. We too can run hot and cold, so affirming and afraid, so much a child of God and a pawn of the devil.

When we hear the rooster's second crow, our weakness sees the light, and we break down. Those tears Peter cried led him back to his Savior. He wasn't the brave, unmovable rock of faith he wanted to be, yet that's what Jesus saw—the rock that He'd chosen to build His church on, able to withstand the gates of Hades. Nothing had changed.

Nothing we can do deletes the words we speak that grieve our Lord. Peter knew that and recommitted all his words from then on to glorify his Lord. He had a choice: give up because of his deep weakness or go on because of Jesus' deeper grace. He chose well.

Lord, thank You for never abandoning me, even when I turn away from You. Please help me recover; help me restart.

START WHERE WE ARE

*Jesus sent out the twelve apostles with
these instructions: "Don't go to the
Gentiles or the Samaritans, but only to the
people of Israel—God's lost sheep."*
MATTHEW 10:5–6 NLT

The first disciples learned all about Jesus' divinity, power, and love from Jesus Himself. Soon it would be time for them to go out and teach on their own. Everyone needed to hear the life-changing truth, but Jesus was specific about their ministry. "Start at home," He told them. "Go to the people you know." He said that for a reason.

Maybe the disciples' heads were full of plans too grand to start with, or maybe they would have lost focus if they were too scattered and far reaching. We can understand. It's easy to get carried away in our zeal. Maybe we want to minister on a big stage, spread God's Word to strangers far and wide. There's nothing wrong with that, and our future may well be full of people and places we can't even imagine yet. But Jesus sets the order.

Let's start with the people we know best. Let us open up all we are in Christ for those closest to us to see.

That can even be harder than witnessing to strangers, but Jesus has prepared us with, not our words, but the Spirit of our Father speaking through us (verse 20) .

We say it all best with a life that imitates Jesus, and the place we call home is the most important place to set an example. The whole world is reached one person at a time. Let's start with one close by.

Lord, please help me bear witness of You to one as if I'm bearing witness to one million.

MISPLACED WORSHIP, REFOCUSED FAITH

"If you are pleased with me, teach me your ways so I may know you and continue to find favor with you."
EXODUS 33:13 NIV

Six weeks. That's how long Moses had been atop Mount Sinai with God. The people at the foot of the mountain grew restless and impatient—the same ones who'd been enslaved in Egypt for four hundred years.

In response to their complaints and disrespect, instead of rallying them on Moses' behalf, his brother and partner in deliverance encouraged them to build a visible "god" and thank it for their freedom. This was the same Aaron that the one true God called to be a priest (Exodus 28:1). We're all subject to pressure from others, and sometimes it breaks us.

To slack in our duties is one thing. To promote the worship of anything other than our almighty God is quite another. We might be tempted to shift the blame the way Aaron did, pointing out those around us who are "evil," but we're responsible for our choices—and leadership—just as he was. And we're all representatives of our God in whatever we do.

The people suffered a plague because of their misguided devotion to a man-made statue, but they came to know God's sovereignty again. Aaron recognized his lapse and asked for forgiveness. God heard Aaron's heart and denoted his priestly responsibility with the budding, blossoming, almond-producing staff that would be "a sign to the rebellious" (Numbers 17:10 NIV). His family priesthood spanned fifteen hundred years.

God doesn't throw away our mission because of our mistakes. He restores us and restates His case. Let us be ready.

Lord, please teach me over and over. Help me learn from my mistakes and use every bit of Your instruction to serve and lead.

A CHANGING BUSINESS MODEL

Everyone, from the least to the greatest, often spoke
of him as "the Great One—the Power of God."
They listened closely to him because for a long
time he had astounded them with his magic.

ACTS 8:10–11 NLT

In Samaria, Simon the sorcerer prospered by tricking people into paying for the "miracles" he performed. But when he heard about Jesus, he believed and stayed with Philip to witness true signs and miracles through faith in the one and only Christ.

Then Peter and John arrived. They helped more followers receive the Holy Spirit, and that was a feat Simon wanted to perform. He reverted to the system he knew, offering money for "God's gift" (Acts 8:20 NLT). Peter cursed the thought. Simon realized that no payment can secure God's blessing and no lack can prevent it.

Simon had become accustomed to paying for everything, and everything he did was for money, so he understood the process of supply and demand. Like Simon, we may see God's grace as an exchange and believe we need to offer up a barter. It may seem more equitable and perhaps easier to understand that way, but as Simon so gratefully learned, the priceless gift of grace is love, not a commodity.

The trader in illusions learned that a heart pure and open, unable and unexpected to pay, was worth more than anything of value in this world. Jesus provides inexhaustible grace and wants nothing we can offer in tangible payment—just everything we have in intangible devotion. That's our exchange, our currency. It's not magic; it's the miracle of our Messiah.

Lord, I know Your grace isn't for sale but given from Your heart. Please make my heart receptive and reflective every day.

GOD'S PROMISED LAND AWAITS

"The LORD your God is the supreme God of
the heavens above and the earth below."
JOSHUA 2:11 NLT

We like to think we'd exhibit great courage under pressure if we had the chance to do something major for God. An unlikely example to follow is a woman who'd traded herself for money yet shows up in the book of Hebrews as one of God's favored.

The Israelites were ready to cross into Jericho. They needed to know what to expect, so spies went to scout the land. Rahab lived in a part of the city wall and knew of the Israelites' victories, their escape from Egypt, and the God they praised for it all. She hid the spies from the king of Jericho, promised more help when they returned, professed her faith in their God, and asked for mercy when they took the city.

The spies were clearly aware of Rahab's lifestyle but offered no condemnation that we know of. Instead they told Joshua about her help and faith, and he sent them to rescue her after the walls of Jericho fell. The

Bible records that Rahab remained with the Israelites (Joshua 6:25).

Sometimes, we feel that the choices we've made disqualify us from God's work, that we'll be ridiculed because of our past, or that we have nothing to contribute. Rahab's faith and boldness obliterated those thoughts with the army of God's grace.

With a focus on the future and trusting God's help to arrive on time, we *can* renounce old ways and do new good. That same courage was evident in Rahab's great-great-grandson David. It's ours for the taking too.

Lord, please give me courage to choose You in all ways, to turn toward a better life, and to trust Your grace to guide me there.

THE BATTLE FOR BETTER

*Since you have heard about Jesus and have learned
the truth that comes from him, throw off your old
sinful nature and your former way of life, which
is corrupted by lust and deception. Instead, let
the Spirit renew your thoughts and attitudes.*

EPHESIANS 4:21–23 NLT

Change is hard. Paul knew that, and he wrote to believers
in Ephesus to remind them that they were no longer
to behave as they had in the past. God had poured
everything good into them and still stood ready to
help them through the challenges every day. Life in
their world called for vigilance, resistance, and faith—a
refusal to return to where they'd been and a readiness
to fight for better.

Those around them who didn't follow Jesus were
no doubt encouraging their bad behavior, and they
were tempted to join in. We may have friends like
that who try to lure us into doing what we shouldn't.
Or maybe sometimes we're the ones luring ourselves?
Even in light of our profession to walk with God, have
we fallen back into old habits and become oblivious

or apathetic to how we're representing Christ? We *can* change. Hard doesn't mean impossible.

Paul said to fight. With "the full armor of God" (Ephesians 6:11 NIV), we're to stand our ground on Him alone. Something is always there to pull us back to habits and desires Jesus has already delivered us from. So He's equipped us with His daily graces and made us full of all the fighting power we need so that no one leads us backward. They'll try continuously, but we stand, fight, and get better at the battle every day.

Lord, please help me follow You and fight everything that doesn't so that I might be an example to others.

I'M DONE. . .WAIT, MAYBE NOT!

Elijah was afraid and fled for his life. He went to Beersheba, a town in Judah, and he left his servant there. Then he went on alone into the wilderness, traveling all day. He sat down under a solitary broom tree and prayed that he might die. "I have had enough, Lord," he said. "Take my life."

1 Kings 19:3–4 nlt

Elijah. So powerful and successful in working for God but just as human as the rest of us. He was burned out, feeling alone and overpowered. Despite Elijah's fatigue and self-doubt, God wasn't worried about His warrior. He comforted him and prepared him for what was to come. "Then the angel of the Lord came again and touched him and said, 'Get up and eat some more, or the journey ahead will be too much for you'" (1 Kings 19:7 nlt).

Sometimes our work is to begin again, or maybe it's to complete a transition. No matter what, God forgives our stumbles and strengthens us for the journey.

Even with the best of intentions, we can't do everything on our own. When we know we need help, God

in His wisdom and grace has already prepared the way ahead. God sent Elijah to "anoint Elisha son of Shaphat from the town of Abel-meholah" to serve as Elijah's replacement and God's new prophet (verse 16 NLT). *"Don't get discouraged, don't give up,"* He says to us. *"Help is on the way."*

That feeling of aloneness and abandonment makes us want to give up and keeps us focused on our lack instead of our fullness. God is near and fixes it all with His grace.

Lord, help me understand that my ache to give up is soothed by Your constant care and perfect planning.

WHEN HE SEES US

When Jesus came by, he looked up at Zacchaeus and called him by name. "Zacchaeus!" he said. "Quick, come down! I must be a guest in your home today."

LUKE 19:5 NLT

Zacchaeus was a rich tax man who overcharged his own Jewish people for taxes demanded by the Roman occupying forces. But he was willing to risk it all to get near the Jewish teacher—even climbing a tree to get a better view. His focus was finally where it should be. He saw Jesus on His way through the town of Jericho, and more importantly, Jesus saw him.

The people Zacchaeus had cheated complained about Jesus befriending Zacchaeus, whom they considered unworthy, but they missed something important: what happened to Zacchaeus is what happens to us all. Jesus' grace doesn't leave us the way it finds us. Our willingness to let grace transform us puts Jesus there in our house too.

Zacchaeus didn't let his past determine his future except to make amends. He vowed to pay back four times what he'd cheated. Because of his commitment to follow Jesus and to follow through with his restoration of wrongs, the short tax collector lives today as a tall example to us. No doubt ashamed of what he was, he accepted Jesus' grace to make him into something else, and he would do his part. He started where he was, and Jesus said that was enough.

None of us can change the past, but all of us can change the future. Repentance leads to redemption—and we are seen forevermore.

Lord, thank You for the opportunity to fix what I've broken. Help me see the riches in following You.

EXCEPT IS A VERY BIG WORD

Elisha replied to her, "How can I help you? Tell me, what do you have in your house?" "Your servant has nothing there at all," she said, "except a small jar of olive oil." Elisha said, "Go around and ask all your neighbors for empty jars. Don't ask for just a few."
2 KINGS 4:2–3 NIV

The widow in the story asked Elisha for help. She came to the prophet after her husband had died, afraid that her sons would be taken as slaves to the Moabites because she had no way to pay her husband's debt. She was frantic, lost in unspeakable despair. But she was about to know God's unrelenting grace.

"Get a lot of jars from your neighbors," Elisha told her. "Go home and fill the jars with the oil you have as long as it lasts." And she did. Even though the instructions were clear, she may have doubted the result. I can imagine having the same doubts, but she was bold and obedient, likely praying as she poured. She filled *all* the jars.

Let's take inventory of all we have and discount nothing, no matter how small, because it's all God needs.

Let's get a lot of jars because a big challenge means a big bounty. Let's shut our door and work, obeying God's instructions. Let's make room for more. It was never the plan for the widow to keep every drop of oil God supplied. The oil was simply a part of the provision, meant to be used so that He could provide even more.

That's how grace works.

Lord, I could always admit defeat—except for You! Let's get a lot of jars and let blessings overflow.

REMEMBER WHO WE ARE

*God has given each of you a gift from his
great variety of spiritual gifts. Use them well
to serve one another. . . . Do it with all the
strength and energy that God supplies.*

1 PETER 4:10–11 NLT

The believers in what is now Turkey felt forsaken and
were suffering hardship. They were struggling to keep
going while living among those who didn't believe. The
Roman government was growing tired of allowing them
to practice their faith. And the division between Jews
and Christians was widening. They began to wonder
if God had abandoned them and was punishing them
somehow for the past they'd left behind, maybe taking
back the gifts they'd been given.

That fear of abandonment is a fear we know too.
We may not face the same persecution today, but all
kinds of things interfere with our faith. And if we're not
careful, those things make us forget the very basis of all
Jesus is—love and faith and grace living forever in our
hearts. He cannot leave us. If He could, He wouldn't

be who He is. And we wouldn't be who we are, gifted and graced to go on.

Whenever the outside world attacks, let us shelter in peace in the soul of Jesus. Let us remember that we are children of the living God. We're forever connected to Him, empowered to turn from our past and change the future with what we become. Armed with His grace, we're forever tethered to Him, learning, loving, and setting the example for those around us. "Most important of all, continue to show deep love for each other, for love covers a multitude of sins" (1 Peter 4:8 NLT).

Lord, help me remember that I'm Yours, once and forever. Let's love with abandon and use up all the gifts You've given me.

RIGHT PLACE, RIGHT HEART

"And who knows but that you have come to your royal position for such a time as this?"

ESTHER 4:14 NIV

In search of a new queen, King Xerxes of Persia chose Esther, an expat, orphan, and worshipper of the exiled God. Mordecai, her older cousin who raised her as his own, told her not to reveal her Jewish heritage because prejudice still existed in the adopted land they called home.

Haman, high official of the king, wanted to destroy all Jews from all the world and convinced the king to issue a decree. When Mordecai learned of the plot, he asked Esther to intervene with the king. Esther was understandably reluctant. Anyone who approached the king unbidden could die, even the queen. But Mordecai must have seen more of God's grace in Esther than she saw in herself, and despite her fear, she discovered her courage. "I will go to the king, even though it is against the law. And if I perish, I perish" (Esther 4:16 NIV).

With bottomless bravery, skilled craftiness, and daring creativity, Esther persuaded the king to bring

Haman to a feast. The king promised to grant Esther a wish, and she revealed herself and asked for the lives of her people. The king agreed and had Haman hanged on the same gallows he'd built to kill his enemy Mordecai.

God's grace changes us, defines us, and empowers us in unlikely situations that become undeniable discoveries of everything within us. I know that despite my fear, with certainty and gratitude, I can trust whatever God's doing around me. Everything I'll need has passed through God's heart to mine.

Lord, please help me recognize the times You've chosen me to help, and make my heart courageous with Your grace.

LOVE, ANSWER, WORK

A third time he asked him, "Simon son of John, do you love me?" Peter was hurt that Jesus asked the question a third time. He said, "Lord, you know everything. You know that I love you." Jesus said, "Then feed my sheep."

JOHN 21:17 NLT

Peter had walked with Jesus, worked at His side, then failed and denied Him. But in quick response to the command of the risen Savior, Peter obeyed and caught another net full of fish. He still knew the love and adoration of his Christ (John 21:7–11). We all know the same love and adoration and are full of the same flaws the early followers were.

When Jesus asked Peter one question three times, the disciple's feelings were hurt. But Jesus wanted him to be truly sure of what he was pledging because He knew the tough life ahead would require complete devotion: the pasture was full of needy sheep, and there was no expedient gate out of the pasture for the one shepherding them.

Instead of being hurt if Jesus asks us something more than once, let us hear and heed exactly what He's saying. The lesson wasn't lost on Peter. He remembered the sheep analogy and used it later when writing to scattered believers with jobs to do. "Be shepherds of God's flock. . .watching over them" (1 Peter 5:2 NIV). Peter made the commitment, and God gave him the strength to live it. He didn't have time for hurt feelings anymore—he was too busy tending the herd.

Lord, help me see that my answers to Your questions are a comfort and a guide.

VOWS BROKEN, GENEALOGY PRESERVED

"And may the LORD give you descendants by this young woman who will be like those of our ancestor Perez, the son of Tamar and Judah."

RUTH 4:12 NLT

Customs of long ago can be hard for us to understand. In biblical times when a brother died, a childless widow was given to the next brother in line. Judah failed to follow that practice with his daughter-in-law Tamar, so she disguised herself as a prostitute and slept with him as he was on his way to Timnah to shear his sheep. For payment, Judah offered to send her a goat from his flock, and she secured his seal and cord and staff as collateral.

When the pregnant Tamar surprised Judah with proof of her child's father, Judah understood and vowed not to make matters worse. "'She is more righteous than I am, because I didn't arrange for her to marry my son Shelah.' And Judah never slept with Tamar again" (Genesis 38:26 NLT).

Instead of being burned to death, which was Judah's first plan, Tamar delivered twin sons Perez and Zerah.

Her time of shame was over. Her part in Israel's heritage had begun. Firstborn Perez was the ancestor of Boaz, who was revered by the people of Jerusalem when he announced he was marrying Ruth. And God did indeed bless their descendants all the way to Jesus.

Judah, Tamar, us—we all skirt the rules, make deals, and plot schemes when we feel pressured and alone. Somehow God finds a way to use even our imperfect means to move His perfect plan forward. His grace overcomes our ego.

Lord, help me choose the right way, and when I don't, help me mend what I've broken and see Your will achieved.

BOLD IN THE DARK, BOLD IN THE LIGHT

There was a man named Nicodemus, a Jewish religious leader who was a Pharisee. After dark one evening, he came to speak with Jesus.
JOHN 3:1–2 NLT

As a member of the supreme council of the Sanhedrin, Nicodemus had a good life. The legalistic Pharisees naturally looked to him to combat that radical preacher in the streets who paid little attention to their beloved laws and relied on mercy and grace instead. And Nicodemus could have led the attack, but something was wrong in his world. Something conflicted with his teaching and tugged at his heart to know more. Despite the risk, he had to find some answers.

"Believe in the God who loves you enough to send Me," Jesus told him (see verse 16). The simple, beautiful, and loving picture of the God he thought he knew confounded Nicodemus more. . .while the world he commanded pulled him away. Nicodemus didn't live the newfound belief out loud during the remainder of Jesus' ministry, but the revelation within was ready to explode like a fractured water balloon. And at Jesus' death, he traded in his comfort for his conviction.

Nicodemus was there at the crucifixion and later helped bury Jesus with the help of Joseph of Arimathea, another reclusive believer who found the courage to ask Pilate for His body (John 19:38). Finally wearing their faith on the outside, they were timid no more. They had changed, and the mercy and grace of Christ became their message to their friends the Pharisees.

Lord, please make me unashamed to make my allegiance to You known in the light, that it may cause bravery in others as well.

WHEN WE MISS, GOD RE-AIMS

"Do not be afraid of them," the LORD said to
Joshua, *"for I have given you victory over them."*
JOSHUA 10:8 NLT

Israel's entry into the promised land had been a long and
costly trek. People from the surrounding area, including
those of Ai, didn't welcome the Israelites, but God had
a plan. Joshua did just as God commanded, and he and
his army overtook and burned the entire city.

Following the success, Joshua renewed the people's
covenant with the one true God, building an altar of
"uncut stones" (Joshua 8:31 NIV)—a plain and simple
testament in contrast to the pagans' altars of bril-
liantly carved images of their useless gods. Only true
faith matters.

But then Joshua's conviction took a small detour. All
other kings in the area wanted war except for the people
of Gibeon to the north. Even they knew that God had
told the Israelites to wipe out all those around them, so
they came up with a different plan in hopes of surviving.
They tricked Joshua into making a treaty and traded
their allegiance for protection. That deal doesn't sound

bad, but Joshua "did not inquire of the LORD" (Joshua 9:14 NIV), and the promise he made to the Gibeonites launched them into war with the Amorites.

Despite Joshua's unilateral decision, God was there to guide the Israelites to victory. The Lord reminded His servant not to be afraid—to focus on that unadorned altar he'd built and remember the power it represented. Joshua's request for a day when the sun would stand still (Joshua 10:12–13) received God's grace, bringing both defeat to the Amorites and salvation for the Gibeonites.

Lord, take away any fear I have that causes me to look away from the uncut depth of Your power.

THE OBEDIENT STORM

A furious squall came up, and the waves broke over the boat, so that it was nearly swamped. Jesus was in the stern, sleeping on a cushion. The disciples woke him and said to him, "Teacher, don't you care if we drown?" He got up, rebuked the wind and said to the waves, "Quiet! Be still!" Then the wind died down and it was completely calm. He said to his disciples, "Why are you so afraid? Do you still have no faith?" They were terrified and asked each other, "Who is this? Even the wind and the waves obey him!"

MARK 4:37–41 NIV

Even the disciples feared for their safety despite being in the presence of the Messiah. They could touch Him, and they still got scared. But at their request, He calmed the wild weather and addressed the real storm in their hearts.

He reminds us today: *"Don't be afraid. Wake Me and I'll comfort you."* That's a lesson we forget in the downpour. And as reassuring as we are to others when their boats are filling up with the sea, when it's our storm, it feels worse, more severe, maybe even too big for Jesus to handle. But no. All storms are the same to Jesus, and so is His grace and power to still them.

If even the wind and waves obey, how can we not? Let's rest on that cushion with Jesus, with quiet faith in the noisy storm. We learn and relearn to call to Him when we're afraid, tempted, sad, confused, lonely—anytime the bad batters our boat—because He is aboard and calms the pain and panic at our request.

Lord, please forgive my fear. Repel with Your protection and grace all that threatens me.

THE END IS ONLY THE BEGINNING

*I have fought the good fight, I have
finished the race, I have kept the faith.*
2 TIMOTHY 4:7 NIV

Law-bound Pharisee to Jesus proclaimer. Paul lived one life in darkness, one in light; one lost to destruction, one founded on grace. That's all of us, because when we find ourselves living in the dark, lost in our ignorance or willful disobedience, we can't go to the light on our own. The road we walk is a dead end until Jesus meets us there. The brighter-than-a-thousand-suns light is only a squint of how far Jesus will go to love us back to Him.

While our own encounter with Jesus may be less dramatic than Paul's, it's no less authentic. Our journey will be less documented but no less true. Let us accept the amazing grace offered and find within it all the strength and power and abilities to carry on and to get over all we leave behind.

Let us not stop when we fail but instead go to God with a repentant heart and receive new grace and direction. This life is only fully lived when we see both sides and choose the way Jesus leads. Paul knew; he lived the darkness into light, proved that the unimaginable is unstoppable because God's plan transforms all that is past into purpose.

Paul ended one horrible existence and began a miraculous life, fought through tests and tragedies to continue the race, and kept his faith and the belief that God's grace is strong, true, and limitless. That has not changed and will not change. God's daily graces are ours too, when we meet and meet again.

Lord, with You, through You, and carried by You, I open my eyes to the road ahead. Let us begin.

DAILY DEVOTIONS TO FEED YOUR SOUL

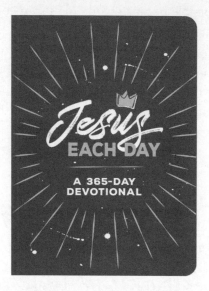

There's no greater personality than Jesus—so why not make time each day to know Him better? This 365-day devotional highlights aspects of Jesus' life and work, His teaching and impact on our lives every day, offering powerful insights as you start or end your day— or for devotional breaks in between.

Flexible DiCarta / 978-1-64352-998-1 / $16.99